The *Practicing Psychic*

An Essential Guide for Staying Grounded, Navigating Skeptics,
and Honoring Your Gift

WILLIAM STILLMAN

Other Books by William Stillman:

Autism and the God Connection

The Soul of Autism

The Autism Prophecies

Conversations with Dogs: A Psychic Reveals What Our Canine Companions Have to Say (And How You Can Talk to Them Too!)

Under Spiritual Siege: How Ghosts and Demons Affect Us and How to Combat Them

The Secret Language of Spirit: Understanding Spirit Communication in Our Everyday Lives

Praise for *The Practicing Psychic*

"As a parapsychologist who has worked with hundreds of mediums, in various states of development over a period of nearly two decades, I have found the need for resources to help guide those people who endeavor to utilize their abilities to work with other people (dead and alive) in a more professional, spiritual, and helpful way. William Stillman's *The Practicing Psychic* nails it! This book is a must-read for anyone delivering messages and insights from Spirit. It gives great clarity and thoughtful consideration to the impact mediums can have on people while working in this field as a professional."

–Mark Allan Keyes, Director of the Pennsylvania Paranormal Association, author and lecturer, and paranormal contributor for Travel Channel's *Paranormal 911* and *Haunted Hospitals*

"There are key elements to being an authentic conduit as well as great responsibilities. In *The Practicing Psychic*, William Stillman has given us a real-world navigation tool and reference guide for working with Spirit and the public."

–Melissa C. Colucci, mediumship and psychometry student

"Never before has a guide been issued encompassing all facets of mediumship for every psychic, both new and established, to hone their talents and morph them into the material world. *The Practicing Psychic* accomplishes this task with a spectacular breakdown of elemental issues and logistics."

–Virginiarose Centrillo, lead psychic medium for the Pennsylvania Paranormal Association, as featured on Travel Channel's *The Haunted* and *Paranormal Survivor*, and metaphysical practitioner of over 35 years

"William Stillman has lovingly and authentically brought together important insights, direction, and examples to help guide you through an often-misunderstood profession. Even the most seasoned practitioner may experience an "Aha!" moment. This book has given me the tools to navigate challenging situations with clients while providing sound business advice and support."

–Marianne Gainey, psychic medium, card reader, reiki master teacher, and owner of Sacred Connections

"Through touching stories and personal experience, William Stillman helps us to understand that to be a good psychic means to *first* be a good person. By revealing how love and gratitude pave the way to personal contentment and supernatural insight, *The Practicing Psychic* serves as a template for how to become a successful psychic or psychic medium."

–Alan B. Smith, host of *Paranormal Now*

First Edition:
First printing

PUBLISHED BY HAUNTED ROAD MEDIA, LLC
www.hauntedroadmedia.com

United States of America

For Sharon, who gave me my start

Table of Contents

Introduction

In 2000, I was working in a rather mundane government position feeling stereotypically undervalued and unappreciated. I was in my late 30s, and coming to understand that my unhappiness, as well as my happiness, started with me. I was not only stuck in a rut professionally but personally. I didn't much care for myself for possessing a rather cynical, judgmental personality—which is odd as I was an intensely sensitive and empathetic child.

When I was young, I recall many strange things happening around me. Some of it was curious but pleasant, like dreaming of picking up scads of pennies out of the grass in my front lawn, and the next day doing just that—on two occasions and in two different locations! And some of it wasn't so pleasant, like the shrouded phantom that would show up in my bedroom doorway each night as I struggled to fall asleep.

Kids tend to be rather socially obtuse until the tween and teen years when most become more sophisticated and aware; cliques may form and people may become more critical of others. Because I was so sensitive, this didn't go over so well with my peers, especially other boys. Nearly every day for many years I was verbally abused, physically harassed, and publicly humiliated. I had no support system of any kind except myself and, unfortunately, I began outwardly reflecting back what others were projecting upon me. I created a hardened shell, a protective façade behind which I was in selfish survival mode and closed off emotionally.

After decades of being in this holding pattern, I felt a calling to aspire higher. Putting this into action required self-assessment, a necessary but sometimes painful accounting of myself. It required confrontation with the truth by embracing the three most powerful words any of us can say of ourselves: I was wrong. Once I acknowledged, to the best of my memory, the various instances in which I had hurt others, the truth was illuminated. There were no more secrets and nothing to hide. Concurrently, I determined to connect to the spiritual wonderment and curiosity I had once experienced. It was only then that I was able to reclaim the aspects of having been a very sensitive little boy. It was only then that I began to harness, tame, and refine my psychic abilities.

Believe it or not, my next step was to quit my job. That may sound irrational or impulsive—and, believe me, I'm not recommending others follow suit—but it was a pivotal moment in my growth. I was debating over what to do, where life would lead me next, and I prayed for an answer. I asked for the answer to be revealed to me in a dream because I thought that would be the most acceptable manner of communication for me. I laid down to take a nap and…nothing happened! But that night, after I had forgotten all about my prayer, I was awakened in the early morning hours with electric current running up and down the length of my body (I've never experienced that sensation before or since). I had just had a vivid, powerful dream full of very distinct imagery that informed me of my future path. I gave notice at work the next day, and have had no regrets ever since.

As I was engaged in this process of emerging and evolving, I desired affirmation for what was unfolding. I was nowhere near the degree of confidence and relaxation I now possess, and was understandably still somewhat anxious with my rather drastic decision. I kept reaching out to other, established psychics but with mixed results. People either didn't respond, and the one or two that did reply suggested I needed a psychic reading which is not what I was wanting. Surprisingly, the only person who responded in kind was an animal communicator with whom I had once worked briefly one summer in 1986! Ultimately, I had to go it alone. But it's been an amazing ride that keeps getting better all the time. Suffice it to say, then, I am completely self-taught in all things spiritual and metaphysical.

Perhaps as a practicing psychic you are fortunate enough to have experienced your gifts and talents consistently throughout your whole life, instead of the very circuitous route I undertook. That is not to say you've been without your own fears and struggles to understand what was manifesting, perhaps even more so. (These things can be challenging, if not overwhelming, to a child trying to balance home and school and childhood in general.) In 2004, I took a leap of faith and "auditioned" for the owner of a local wellness center. She saw the glimmer of something there and gave me a chance to work for her. And I haven't looked back. Maybe you are in similar circumstances, operating out of a holistic studio or wellness center; or perhaps you operate solo, setting up at new age faires and expos, or providing readings via phone or internet platforms.

This volume is not intended to be a how-to guide for the curious novice to develop psychic abilities, as there are plenty of those books to be found. Instead, I desired to craft a handbook of sound advice for the psychic already practicing his or her craft. If the physicians' Hippocratic Oath can be distilled to "First, do no harm," then perhaps professionals in my field could benefit from a book of best practices. Such a guidebook might prove valuable, especially as it seems there are more and more casual, full- and part-time psychics than ever before. To that end, my goal in composing this book has been to offer a code of ethics by which to preserve the integrity of our collective endeavors. You may not personally align with all of it but my hope is that, professionally, it will resonate as valid and authentic advice.

Part 1

Nuts
and
Bolts

Chapter 1

Cultivating Confidence

A quick reality check before we delve into the greater discussion: What is your motivation for wanting to work professionally as a psychic or a psychic medium? Is it because you want the adulation of others telling you how amazing you are? Is it the satisfaction of proffering intuitive information that will shock and awe? Or perhaps it is because you have felt maligned and unappreciated and this is a way for you to feel superior, special, or above average. If any of the preceding rationales are your incentive for being in this very specialized field, get out now! None of these reasons are authentic, and if your desire is to both amaze others while elevating yourself then you've got it all wrong. Working as a reputable psychic actually requires that you divorce yourself from ego in order to focus on your clientele. The only authentic incentive for committing to this work is because you have discerned how to employ your spiritual gifts and talents in a manner that serves others. Period. So, if you've got it, great! If you don't got it, you can cultivate the confidence necessary to "get it." But it does require that you get out of your own way (that's the interference of ego again!). Remember: It's not about you, it's about what you have to offer others. Also always remember: It doesn't come *from* you, it comes *through* you. You will see this theme repeated throughout this book, and believing in it will aid in keeping you humble.

It is, however, easy to feel unsure about the extent of your gifts. To really thrive in this field, you've got to be good at what you do. To the paying client, that means that you are accurate and authentic. You're only as good as your last reading, your last workshop, or your last group event. Why? Because word travels fast, especially in this day and age of online outlets and social media platforms by which you may be rated and critiqued. Praiseful word-of-mouth is what will sustain you and your practice. It is your bread and butter if you see this work as a sustainable career path. Very few people can earn a living doing it, but don't allow that to daunt you; let it inspire you to persevere!

There are a number of things that should be in place in order for you to move forward successfully. None of this is rocket science. All of it is easily attainable, but does requires your time, attention, and discipline. If you're serious about earning income as a psychic, you've got to do your homework. That means behind-the-scenes preparation before you even get to the point of sitting with a single client, starting with assessing whether you are well enough to accept responsibility for doing this work in the first place. And it is a tremendous responsibility. You have to remember: we're talking about people's lives and lost loved ones. They are coming to you seeking answers, healing, and closure. You have to feel able to professionally yet compassionately deliver on their hopes.

I've met a lot of folks in this field, and adjunct fields such as reiki, massage, and other healing modalities, who, in my opinion, have absolutely no business attempting to heal or otherwise administer to others. Why? Because they, themselves, are not well. I'm not suggesting that they are disingenuous or aren't well intentioned in the services they desire to provide. But you have to remember that there is great potential for folks like you and I to attract clients who are not well either. They may be severely depressed. They may be grieving a significant loss. They may be in the throes of a bitter divorce. They may experience chronic physical pain. They may be tolerating an abusive relationship. Or they may have worries about a loved one who is struggling with addiction.

I have also identified all of the preceding traits in would-be practitioners themselves. As such, they are at-risk of manifesting two situations. First, know that like attracts like. There may be no benefit to the service being provided because neither practitioner nor client is well and healthy. So, the exchange, in essence, gets cancelled out and has little to no effect. Second, oftentimes people who are not well and healthy are carrying with them "attachments," as you may already well know. These attachments are comprised of heavy, negative energy that may actually latch onto you, in essence, hitchhiking home with you and affecting you and those with whom you live (including pets). Such attachments serve to erode your well-being, causing mental confusion and fatigue, while depleting your energy.

Given the foregoing, suffice it to say that to optimally best serve others who are seeking you for intuitive guidance and direction, you must first be fit yourself. And that requires a conscious balancing of three domains, or three aspects of your personhood, on a daily basis. The three domains are: mental-emotional well-being, physical well-being, and spiritual well-being. Indeed, it is also these three domains that may deteriorate; the erosion resulting from the infiltration of unchecked negative energy. Think about it: Have you ever been in the company of someone and, afterwards, come away feeling "dirty," almost like you need to bathe? Or, similarly, have you also come away feeling agitated, drained or even depressed? These experiences could well be due to the unwanted transfer of toxic negative energy from that person to yourself. (How to deal with this will be discussed shortly.) Minimize the potential to be affected unaware by strengthening your fitness across the three domains: mental-emotional well-being, physical well-being, and spiritual well-being.

Where your mental-emotional well-being is concerned, consider how you maintain yourself. You should definitely lean toward being an optimistic, glass-half-full type of individual, especially if you're going to be in a position to counsel others who are seeking help, guidance, or closure. Creating mental-emotional balance may be challenging because—by our very nature—psychics are extra-sensitive and, therefore, more prone than average to be emotionally affected by what we see and hear around us. In fact, that may be the best place to start: being mindful of the media to which you allow yourself to be exposed. What does this mean for you, personally? Only you can determine this, as it is not a one-size-fits-all approach.

Take social media, for example. It will be beneficial for you to have a social media presence, maybe even in addition to a formal web site (this will be discussed in Chapter Seven). But to what extent is your time otherwise consumed by social media, following others, and monitoring (and commenting) on the remarks or diatribes of others? I am a baby boomer and, to be honest, not a huge fan of modern technology. Believe it or not, I don't even use a cell phone! I don't want the distraction of what seems like a colossal waste of time and energy for so many other people. A lot of social media can be offensive and inflammatory. Do you really want to get into it, firing back and forth, with someone on a social media platform right before you're scheduled to go into an appointment? The risk of being unable to compartmentalize by separating out your own ego may be difficult. If you are actively using social media, decide how much, or how little, is manageable for you so that you can devote the time to good mental-emotional hygiene.

Next, I don't think it's possible to be an authentic psychic if you cheat and lie regularly. Note I said "authentic" psychic. There have been people who have portrayed themselves as psychics and were clearly charlatans and hustlers who were flat-out cheating and lying to their clients. I recall hearing about a local fella who decided to earn some extra cash and made it known through his network of contacts that he was now in the business of conducting psychic readings when, in fact, he was gathering information about people from their social media accounts and using the information to mesmerize and manipulate them. If you operate in this manner, it will catch up to you before long; you can't consistently fleece people paying good money without eventual repercussions. As it happened, this guy was called out for his fraudulent scheme, but this unethical behavior absolutely gives the rest of us honest folks a bad reputation. This is even more incentive, then, to conduct oneself with honesty and integrity. Personally, I don't lie at all, not even what other people call "white lies." It's just not part of my repertoire and it's exhilarating to have no worries about remembering untruths to preserve an aura of being genuine because I'd like to think I already am. Liars always have to keep track of their lies, and that is not only exhausting, it's destructive.

Similarly, consider the language you use in everyday conversation. How much of it is critical and judgmental of others, even to making comments about people on television or in videos? What kind of remarks are you making on social media? And how often do you curse or swear? As a general rule, I don't curse or swear—although I occasionally relapse because I'm human, but it's not something I do routinely in the way that every other word is a four-letter one for some people. I don't like such coarse and uncivilized language and it's particularly disconcerting for me to hear it being used in anger.

Language matters, and words carry weight and influence that can hurt or heal. Those who argue, "It's just words" aren't taking into account the oftentimes demeaning and destructive *emotion* with which the language is used. When people swear, it can be done for humorous effect but most often it is used for emphasis to communicate anger, degradation, and disgust—all of which is counterproductive to becoming mentally-emotionally fit and authentic. So if you've been known to curse with the best of them, weigh your words carefully and measure what it is you're "putting out there."

Where your mental-emotional well-being is concerned, you'll also want to be cautious for what it is that you permit yourself to be exposed to in terms of viewing material. For myself, this means no zombies, no horror movies, no true-crime shows that reenact horrific murders in graphic detail—I don't wish to be tainted or influenced by the darkness associated with any of it. It's really something how quickly we can become desensitized to watching people committing really brutal acts against others or themselves. Perhaps you are a bit more resilient and can put some measure of popular entertainment in a proper perspective that suits your lifestyle but it's definitely not my cup of tea. (And thank goodness the trend of horror movies that included agonizing scenes of gratuitous torture seems to have cycled out.) This also goes for the very violent video games that may be enjoyed by you or even someone else living in the same household. A lot of video games are not cartoonish but are amazingly realistic in making you feel you are there as an active participant. A good rule of thumb is, if anything you've been exposed to rattles you, causes you to lose sleep, or affects your thoughts days after the fact, be sure to add it to your list of things to avoid so that your domain of mental-emotional well-being remains stabilized.

Equally important is the domain addressing your physical well-being. Why? Because it correlates precisely with the mental-emotional domain. Understand that what you think and feel has a direct impact on how you feel physically. Ever notice that optimistic, positive-thinking people don't get sick very often, or can manage illness with a keener navigation than the average individual? They seem to recuperate much more quickly and easily. They also don't seem to show signs of aging as others do. Conversely, have you noticed that people who are chronic complainers and pessimists are more frequently sick, or their illnesses linger or beget more ongoing illness? (The latter group are the same people who seem to attract bad luck wherever they go, or don't understand why every device they touch malfunctions.) There's a reason these dichotomies of personality may approach (and heal) the same physical setback differently: attitude. Attitude matters in part because optimism grants a degree of immunity against mental and physical illnesses

Would you believe I have witnessed people who have worked themselves into cancer? These same people are not only pessimists who seem to criticize and complain as often as they breathe. They are simply not effective stewards of their own bodies. Suffice it to say, their unhealthy mental-emotional state of mind has affected their physicality. Not that folks of this regard seem to care either; they tend to be smokers, gamblers, overeaters, alcoholics, and so on. But these same individuals repeatedly lapse into portraying themselves as victims, moaning about the ongoing bad luck they've been dealt in life. The irony is that, more often than not, they have *created* the very circumstances about which they are complaining! And if they haven't created it, it has found them by virtue of attracting negative energy.

Negative energy knows a sucker when it sees one and decides to prey upon the vulnerable and miserable by setting up shop *in the person's body*. This attachment perpetuates "dis-ease" and chronic unwellness. The majority of this could be reversed by tending to one's body with great care and deliberation in the spirit of *prevention* not *intervention*. This means taking precautions and treating your body wisely *now* to prepare for longevity in good health. I suspect I am very unusual, but—to date—I have never been seriously ill, have never had a broken bone, have never been hospitalized, have never had an operation of any kind, nor have I ever been involved in a serious accident. That may sound quite rare for someone of my seasoned years, but then I am also mindful of caring for my physical well-being on a daily basis. Why? Because this is all in keeping with desiring to be as clear and pure a channel as possible. Psychic input can be optimally aided by how clean you keep your "house."

Physical well-being, for me, requires that I don't drink alcohol or smoke. I've never touched an illegal substance in my life. I have some orange juice with my breakfast and then only *ever* drink water, if you can believe it. I've had a vegetarian diet exclusively since 1995, and I exercise daily, which means long walks, 50 pushups each morning, and I work out with weights. So, in essence, I am in bootcamp each day with respect to caring for my mental-emotional and physical well-being because, in my opinion, that's territory that comes with the job. But what works for me may not necessarily be what works for you. If you can eat what you want, rarely exercise, and have no filters with respect to what you do and say, *and* can maintain spot-on authenticity as a psychic—more power to you! Others among you may simply not have the kind of time it takes to invest in so diligent a lifestyle because you are working at a job that pays the bills, you have small children, you're caring for a family member, or you are preoccupied elsewhere. That's fine too, but remember that you'll get out of it only so much as you put into it. If you consider being a practicing psychic an avocation or something you do infrequently and part-time, then that approach may work for you. It is entirely your call. Again, this is what works for me.

The third and final domain is spiritual well-being. I was raised in the Episcopal church and now consider myself to be a non-denominational Christian. When I pray, I pray to God because that is how I was taught from early childhood on. I use the word "God" because it is the term with which I am most comfortable, and I am unapologetic about it. My belief system may not be your belief system, and that's okay. But I will remain firm in stating unequivocally that you cannot do work that employs your spiritual gifts and talents and not have a connection with a Higher Power. It is in keeping with the mantra, "It doesn't come from you, it comes *through* you." I express gratitude and appreciation to God in prayer throughout each day, usually at times of solitude, such as on my walks, working out, or while driving en route to work. I never listen to music while engaged in these activities so I can focus my attention fully. The intentional investment in the upkeep of your mental-emotional and physical well-being, blending with your spiritual well-being, serves to heighten your overall vibrational frequency in attunement with the higher vibrational frequencies you seek to access as an authentic psychic. Simply put, it is consistent balancing of mind, body and spirit. Believe me, God has your back and *wants* you to succeed by manifesting your gifts to serve others.

Personally, I don't care if you don't use the word God. Perhaps you are of another religious persuasion or spiritual belief system that owes reverence to another omnipotent entity or energy. In fact, I'm discovering more and more that a lot of young people don't use the word God, instead favoring words like "Source," "Universe," "Spirit" or "Higher Power." Again, you can call it Wonder Woman for all I care. I just know that I would be unable to do what I do to the degree of accuracy and authenticity I have been blessed to receive if I didn't honor the source of it all. Which leads into my next point in the cultivation of your confidence.

You have—assigned to you and exclusively you—an ambassador on behalf of all that it right and true and good and kind. It is your primary Spirit Guide. Perhaps you are already in direct communication with this foremost and ethereal concierge. A surprising number of people who are "readers" of one kind or another, and those who are aspiring psychics, are not connected to their Guide. In my opinion, discovering and making active good use of this resource is crucial to your work as a psychic. I would not be able to do what I do without my "team" of Spirit Guides. Engaging with them is simpler than you might think if you haven't already.

I wish to stress the importance of always connecting to, and communicating with, your Spirit Guide in the context of a prayer or a blessing. This protects you and exponentially increases the likelihood that what comes next will be authentic. Remember, if you are so far along in your spiritual development to be calling upon your Guide or Guides, it means you are also vulnerable to setbacks. There are negative and ill-intended energies out there that wish to intercept your ability to manifest your gifts and talents, cause you to relapse, and cause you to be ineffectual in your endeavors by becoming derailed and distracted. They will masquerade as something they are not in order to gain your trust. They can, in fact, claim to be Guides, angels, or even deceased loved ones. Commit to due diligence by protecting yourself properly in advance of all communications with your Guides.

The first step is to christen your Guide with a name of your choosing. Try to sense if your Guide is male or female. Perhaps your Guide will show itself in animal form or as some other way of being other than human. The name is not so much as important as the acknowledgment of the Guide's presence. Honestly, they don't care what we call them; they care about the *relationship*. On occasion, there can be synchronicities related to the Spirit Guide's identity however. More than once, I've had a Spirit Guide tell a client, through me, that the Guide had been their imaginary childhood playmate and mentioned making mud pies or having tea parties, which the clients were able to confirm. Another time, I told a client that her Spirit Guide's name was Bernadette and she gasped, saying she had always been attracted to that name! Most recently, a client's Spirit Guide, whom we identified as Delilah in a previous session, expressed how tickled she was that he was wearing her name. Sure enough, he was wearing a football hoodie with the word "Philadelphia" across his chest. Delilah, of course, may be spelled using letters found in Philadelphia!

Once you christen your Guide, pay attention for roughly a week to ten days out. You should receive a validation of the Guide's presence. This may manifest in you personally sensing a presence (which should never be frightening or discomforting). You may also feel as though your intuitive abilities have ramped up. You may encounter your Guide in a vivid dream, prayer or meditation. You may also receive validation of the name you gave your Guide. For example, my primary Guide is "Frank." It was just a name that popped into my head when I was considering what to call him.

A week later, there was a knock at my door and, when I answered it, there stood a young man in his twenties. He was driving the garbage truck that pulled into my cul-de-sac and, as he was backing out, he damaged my mailbox post. He was coming to the door to tell me. I supposed that the sanitation company would pay for a replacement post but he offered to do it himself. When he gave me his contact information, I realized his name was Frank and his last name—Ward—is a word in the English language that pertains to guardianship and the act of keeping guard. His name translated succinctly to: Frank the Guardian! Not only that, when he honored his word and replaced the post, he told me he wasn't supposed to have been there the day of the damage—he was filling in for someone who called out sick and it was his first time driving in my area! The symbolism of this young man was obvious and, afterwards, I began to connect to Frank, my Guide, undeniably and effortlessly.

I wish to conclude this chapter by emphasizing the importance of proper protection in your work. Prior to interacting with any clients, I bless the space in which I will be working by saying the Lord's Prayer. I illuminate every corner of the space with the light of the truth. I next bless all who enter the space. I then cast a veil of protection overtop of, and surrounding, the space. The veil is a glorious golden shield fashioned out of luminous light. It will insulate and encapsulate; it will defend and protect; and it will repel and deflect anything that is not for the greater good of the highest order.

Next, I tap the center of my forehead, or third eye, three times to signify that I am officially "turned on." I then call forth my Spirit Guides, individually and by name, and ask that they descend their vibrational frequency in order to meet me a minimum of half way. I ask that they work carefully and compassionately with me so that I might render good service to all who seek truth through me. I then ask for assistance to pace myself so that my energy is apportioned equally and that each receives his or her own, without hemorrhaging all of my own personal reserve of energy.

Next, I ask to be divorced from ego so that I might experience self-forgetfulness, a state of being in which one becomes less aware of one's own physicality and more aware of oneness with the Universe. I then grant permission for the soul energy of loved ones related to, or loved by, each client to come forward through me serving as the mouthpiece, voice-box, and spokesperson for the duration of time that I am in the space and so long as it is helpful, healing, and humorous. Finally, I say a blessing with each client before we officially begin his or her psychic reading. Combine these practices with my daily regime and you can appreciate how immersed I am in spiritual bootcamp each day, training as if preparing as a tri-athlete or a concert violinist!

Enacting this process clearly sets my intentions before I proceed with any sort of work, and it offers me the protection I require in order to feel quite solid and confident moving forward. You may enact a similar ritual in order to prepare. Your routine may include clearing your workspace with sage. You may burn incense or candles. You may enter into a meditative trance. Or you may arrange crystals or other stones in an energetic pattern to benefit your intuition. I would never discourage you from any of these, or other, useful actions if such preparations aid you in feeling confident. But, in my opinion and in my experience, these are all extraneous activities. Bottom line is, nothing trumps the power of your genuine, sincere, and heartfelt prayers. It is your birthright as a human being, and it is your direct line to the Higher Power with which you will be collaborating.

In fact, your prayer is precisely what makes the distinction between that which is a function of your own everyday imagination, and receiving spiritual input from a divine source. I cannot stress this enough; once you set your intentions in a grounded, gratitude-filled prayer, you are no longer working alone. You have called in the spiritual troops for support, and what you will be communicating to others holds the greatest likelihood of being accurate and authentic. I know of no better way of feeling confident in my own work in which client expectations are high, and in which I am expected to pluck relevant information about a total stranger seemingly out of thin air.

Chapter 2

Do What You Are

What are you? If you're already earning some sort of income in this field, then you've got to define yourself so potential clients know in advance what to expect of a session with you. Are you a psychic? Are you a psychic medium? Or are you both? There's a significant difference between the two, as you may already know. A psychic is someone who is able to provide intuitive information, advice, and guidance pertaining to someone's general health, welfare, and well-being and that of their loved ones (who are still living), including pets. A psychic might offer predictions about romantic relationships; travel, moving, and relocation; perspective on someone's children; and someone's future financial picture. A psychic might also suggest ways to improve oneself through appropriate lifestyle changes, or by identifying dormant gifts and talents to be developed. People seek out psychics to affirm, validate, or refute their own intuitive hunches; the healthiest of those folks then weigh their options, taking into account whatever the psychic has predicted before determining their next course of action.

On the other hand, a psychic medium can provide all of the preceding services *and* possesses the ability to channel, or communicate directly with, and speak on behalf of, deceased people related to, or known by, the client. This ability goes beyond offering basic, intuitive information about a client's deceased loved ones such as their birth month or favorite color. If you are a true psychic medium, as a matter of course, you are able to provide what is called *evidential mediumship* in which you are relaying highly random yet very specific bits of information known only to your client and the deceased individual.

For example, I was sitting with a female client who was asking to connect with her sister who had passed on. I heard music in my head, and asked my client if the 1970 song "Close to You" by Burt Bacharach (and famously sung by The Carpenters) meant anything to her. She replied that, yes, indeed it did—growing up, she and her sister had a teddy bear that *played that very song* when you squeezed its paw and they would take turns doing this with each other. In fact, she still had the bear stored in a box in her basement! Recalling the musical teddy bear as a reference connecting my client to her sister was probably the furthest thing from her mind. But the validity of conveying this unusual and obscure bit of minutiae on behalf of her deceased sister made it all the more powerful for being so unexpected. And, obviously, there was no prior way for me to have known this either.

In another instance, I was sitting with a young fella in his twenties. Even as I was saying my blessing with him, a male spiritual presence came through chomping at the bit. In fact, before we had officially begun the session, I asked this young man if he knew another young male who passed very suddenly and he indicated yes. Once I finished my blessing, the presence stepped forward, kissed this young man on the side of his cheek, and called him "brother." My client burst into tears and confirmed that it was his older brother who had died in an auto accident. I was also shown a black crow, and I asked him, "What's Black Crow?" I was thinking perhaps it was a reference to The Black Crowes, the rock band. But my client told me that his brother had alcohol dependency issues and Black Crow was actually a dark rum that one drinks in shots. His brother drank it, among others. It was a reference to his brother's alcoholism, what facilitated his crash, and also a precaution for the surviving brother (my client) to avoid the example set by the deceased brother. The brother also referenced an auto repair shop, and my client affirmed that both he and his brother were mechanics and had hoped to have their own garage. His brother was projecting the possibility of my client not only having a garage but I was also shown the business sign included "...and Son," indicating the child my client had yet to bear! The session served as a powerful validation, and my client walked out a believer in addition to feeling empowered for the future.

A psychic medium may also—casually and subtly—demonstrate aspects of the deceased individual's personality such as imitating his or her body language by adopting posture, gestures, and facial expressions. The medium may also use words or phrases typical of the deceased individual being channeled, such as the time a client's father referred to his blue jeans as "dungarees" and said he had been unfaithful to her mother for having "hot nuts." This should be effortless, and should not be intrusive, disruptive, or unnerving to the medium; it should be temporary so long as the psychic session is active. Sometimes, if I am channeling an elderly loved one, they'll use slang terminology that has become all but obsolete, such as when they tell a client that she has "moxie," a word synonymous with spunk, gumption, and stubborn determination. Conversely, if I am channeling a younger person, I may take on some of their more contemporary slang, which leads me to my next point.

You'll recall me previously stating that, as a general rule, I don't curse or swear. But that doesn't mean that my clients' deceased loved ones also didn't curse or swear! I have on many occasions been embarrassed by sheepishly conveying word-for-word the colorful curse words of others. One client's deceased brother said, through me, that he would've thought going to a psychic was "a real shitshow" when he was alive! That's not a phrase that I've ever used, but my client validated that it was exactly what her brother would have remarked.

If you are not comfortable repeating verbatim someone's bad language, you are certainly within your rights to censor it by relaying the information in your own phraseology. For me, I understand that when clients' deceased loved ones speak this way, it is one form of spiritual shorthand; that is, a quick and easy way to demonstrate an aspect of his or her (usually his) personality that a client would know to immediately recognize as Uncle Joe, dad, their best friend, and so on. It is otherwise harmless so long as it is being communicated in a manner that is joking, teasing, or self-effacing. More than one repentant father has come through saying, "Sorry I was such an asshole." If the cursing is angry, accusatory, or cynical, that's not a good thing and we'll discuss more about that later on.

The preceding examples should aid you in deciding if you are a psychic or a psychic medium. If you decide you are, at present, a psychic, it does not mean you can't become a psychic medium. You certainly have a good foundation from which to build and develop the skills necessary to channel the soul energies of clients' deceased loved ones. In fact, it took me some time before I embraced the term "psychic medium" for feeling it was quite a lofty responsibility—and it is. Once you begin identifying yourself as a psychic medium, you immediately elevate all prospective clients' expectations to bring forth proof of their deceased loved ones' presence in a manner that is authentic and evidential. Thus, the bar gets set very high. Be sure you are ready, willing, and able to bear this level of responsibility. It is a serious matter as we are talking about other people's lost loved ones—some of whom passed suddenly and tragically—and with that can come tremendous guilt and grief. As this is not a how-to book, I will not be instructing you on how to become a medium but I am confident that there are other resources which you may access in order to more fully develop your potential in this area.

As a psychic medium, it is important to understand that not all spiritual energy is of the same frequency, capacity or capability. This may be difficult to understand, especially for the layperson who just wants to connect to a very specific individual; to them, it's all the same. But, as you know, each soul energy is a unique personality type. As such, there are variables that can influence your ability to tap into a certain deceased loved one. This includes the desire and strength of the individual's soul energy to present itself in that very moment. Just like in life, some souls have "bigger" personalities than others. I've been in countless situations in which a deceased relative came barreling through even though it was the last person from whom my clients would have expected to hear. If a client is willing to accept this and roll with it, oftentimes a more recalcitrant, quieter or passive personality will eventually come forward—and it is usually the very person with whom they were hoping to connect.

In order for you to be at your best when communicating the intuitive impressions you are receiving, you should distinguish the methods by which it comes to you. Being psychic is essentially possessing a magnification of one or more of your human senses (hence the phrase "sixth sense" or multisensory when discussing such phenomenon). The best way to know your psychic gifts is to see if you can align them with the "clairs." Doing this will give you a way by which to compartmentalize your gifts and better understand the psychic vehicle or method by which you are most likely to receive information.

For example, I receive information by being impressed with visuals, mental imagery that forms in my head in the way of pictures, movies, words, phrases, and sometimes a name or an initial representing a name. (Clients love it when you get relevant names!) I may be caused to feel something physically, as in my gut. Or I may be caused to smell, hear, or taste something. If you are reading carefully and between the lines, you'll notice that the preceding ways in which I receive my spiritual input correlate to see, feel, smell, hear and taste; or, in other words, an ethereal extension of my human senses. These are the "clairs." Here's a quick example: In channeling a client's grandfather, who helped raise her, I "saw" him in his World War II military uniform; I "felt" emanating from his presence a tremendous sensation of love and adoration for her (and her daughter, whom he did not know); I "smelled" his cigarette smoke; I could "hear" him say to the bartender at the American Legion, to which he had taken her as a child, "How about a Shirley Temple for my little gal here,"; and I could "taste" the birthday cake with pink icing from him and his wife in recognition of my client's birthday less than a week earlier.

Like the term déjà vu, the clairs are all French terms with the clair prefix meaning "clear." Clairvoyance translates to clear seeing or clear vision, that is, the ability to see beyond. Clairvoyants convey intuitive information based upon the visuals they receive. Oftentimes, a clairvoyant will use a device as a point of distraction and focus, such as the classic stereotype of the fortune teller who peers into a crystal ball. The images being received do not manifest *in* the crystal ball, per se; but staring at it (or the prism or the crystal or any other object that serves as a conductor) allows the psychic individual a way to concentrate on his or her own mental imagery.

Again, as you may already know, with clairvoyance, the fleeting imagery you receive is in your mind's eye, and not literally manifesting before your very eyes as a standing vision. I have had to explain to clients that experiencing clairvoyance can be rather vague or ambiguous at times; it is not as crystal-clear as looking at a photograph. Often it is hazy, like looking at something through an atmosphere of fog. So, for example, when I tell a client I'm seeing a dog in Spirit and they ask, "What breed?" I can usually only reply, "I don't know but I know it's a dog that is deceased…" and often I can distinguish the gender. On other occasions, I'm able to nail the breed, but it is all dependent on the will of Spirit and what is intended to be communicated.

Clairaudience is clear hearing. Like clairvoyance, clairaudience is not something you hear externally; it comprises sounds, noises, music, and sometimes voices in your head. Wait—voices in your head? Then what's the difference between someone diagnosed with schizophrenia who experiences auditory hallucinations as one symptom, and the psychic who experiences clairaudience, you may wonder? The difference for you as the psychic is that you control it, it doesn't control you. This means that your clairaudient experience is neither disruptive nor intrusive (as it would be for someone with mental illness), and is confined to the duration of the time you are working as a practicing psychic.

Clairaudience is a quick method for Spirit to communicate a greater concept in a sound byte. For instance, the preceding example of the song "Close to You" was psychic shorthand for a bigger concept beyond merely referencing the teddy bear shared by the two sisters. It concisely communicated that the emotional bond between the two can never be severed and, in the deceased sister's words, she will always be *close to you*. Makes complete sense, doesn't it? Songs are often used by Spirit in such a manner, like the time I heard Adele singing, "Hello from the other side…" which was literal for the client who had recently lost a close friend and who was also an Adele fan. One standard clairaudient communication in my psychic lexicon is when I hear Frank Sinatra singing "My Way." Sometimes this one's a toss-up between meaning that a client's deceased loved one was very particular or even controlling exerting authority over doing it "their way" (logical, right?), and it signifying, literally, that "My Way" was a specific and relevant song for the deceased loved one.

On other occasions, where clairaudience is concerned, I have heard seemingly random sounds that prove to be relevant such as someone coughing, and my client will explain that her father was a heavy smoker. On occasion, I'll hear a gunshot ring out. This could be interpreted in a couple of ways. First, it could indicate that the deceased was a firearm collector or a hunter. Or it could mean that someone was shot (that is, murdered) or that he or she shot themselves. Sometimes I'll perceive a clairvoyant and clairaudient impression *paired together*, like seeing and simultaneously hearing a motorcycle backfire. It may be that I'll also hear a noise associated with a deceased pet. On many occasions, I've heard the sound of a dog's nails clicking on hardwood or tile flooring, for example; or I'll hear the dog dropping or chewing on hard kibble.

I nearly never hear what sounds like actual voices. But the curious thing about that is, I have a small collection of audio recordings that clients have sent me over the years in which there is briefly heard *a third voice* evident upon playback of the recording but which was not heard in real time. I have to wonder how much of this phenomenon influences me on a subliminal or subconscious level. In one audio outtake, for example, I am telling a client to focus on her family, her children, and her work. As I tell her this, I sense that her Spirit Guide has stepped forward to place a reassuring hand on her shoulder and to steady her. Simultaneous with my comment is a sound unlike anything I have ever encountered until I heard the ethereal echo created with crystal singing bowls. The closest thing I can compare the sound to is something along the lines of a musical sigh.

On another occasion, I was tapping into the essence of a client's deceased grandmother. My client was about to embark on fulfilling a dream by launching a new business but was feeling uncertain and nervous about the risk. Translating on behalf of her grandmother, I told her the sorts of encouraging things you might expect a doting grandma to say, such as "How can you fail to succeed?" and "We love you, dearie."—things that, quite frankly, anyone could've made up. But on the playback of the recording, and in the beat right before I say, "And she says, 'We love you, dearie,'" there's a voice that whispers, "And we love you." Again, in this and the preceding example, neither my clients nor I actually heard anything out of the ordinary in the moment although these anomalies were clearly captured on tape. This sort of occurrence really gives you reason to pause and consider just who, or what, may be around us at any given moment. It may also be a subtle form of clairaudience on a whole other level.

Clairsentience, or clear sensing, is a familiar sensation to anyone who is a parent, a pet owner, or has a close relationship with a twin or sibling. Distilled to layperson's terms, it is "mother's intuition," that sixth sense of knowingness—without knowing how you know—that your loved one is in need. It is usually a gut feeling that may be similar to an uneasy apprehension or anxiety that can manifest in physical symptoms of racing heartbeat, quickening pulse, and a slight nausea. Clairsentience has also been experienced by those of us who have impulsively exclaimed, "I just *knew* that was going to happen!" in reaction to some occurrence about which we felt a distinct hunch in advance.

There have been many occasions in which I have simply felt compelled to blurt something out without any pretext; I just know it but don't ask me why or how. This is clairsentience. It is a fleeting impulse that may also feel slightly unpleasant. For example, I have felt the sensation of being stabbed and shot, and, in one instance, I felt something fall over top of me, crushing me under its weight. In these instances, what I was experiencing physically aligned with how the deceased individual, whom I was channeling, passed. The sensation of being crushed occurred when a woman's deceased husband had shelves of bank deposit boxes topple onto him, pinning him, and suffocating him.

Clairalience and Clairgustance are two experiences that often go hand in hand as they relate to our two most powerful senses that correlate with memory. Clairalience is clear smelling and Clairgustance is clear tasting. As with the other clairs, these experiences do not linger indefinitely. The sensations associated with clairalience and clairgustance are very temporary—just enough to communicate their essence. In fact, you may even be caused to question if you really just smelled or tasted what you think you did!

Most often, with clairalience, there will be very distinctive scents that would be immediately recognizable by my clients such as grandma's lilac bush, mother's Chanel No. 5 perfume, or granddad's cigar. As with clairaudience, clairalience is psychic shorthand for conveying a bigger concept deftly and efficiently. This is because the aroma conjures not just memories but *emotions* as well. Oftentimes, the memories are happy and pleasant, and the emotions are joyful and loving. But when I smell alcohol, it is almost always a sign that the deceased had a dependency issue or was, indeed, alcoholic. On occasion, clairalience serves as a symbolic way of communicating something by association in my own memory. Most recently, this happened just before going into psychic reading. I saw and smelled a McDonald's Big Mac hamburger. I asked my client if the name Mac meant anything and she nodded: it was her deceased father's nickname, which was an abbreviation of his surname which began with "Mac."

Oddly enough, there have been occasions on which I have smelled cow manure. Once was a literal communication and another time was a metaphor. Such instances are examples of why no one psychic will ever be 100% spot-on accurate; there will always be a margin of error open to misinterpretation. In the former instance, the manure I detected was because a client's mother grew up on a farm with cows. Not only that, one of my client's treasured photos of her deceased mother is that of mom posed next to a bag of manure. She was dubbed "Manure Mom" by the family! In the other example, a woman's deceased husband came through causing me to smell cow manure but it was to communicate the "bullshit" of the legal delays and stonewalls in holding his workplace accountable for the negligence that led to his accidental death. Sometimes—believe it or not—I'll smell someone's flatulence, and my client will say, "Yup, that's dad alright!"

In the best-case scenario, Clairgustance is experienced with brief food-related tastes on the tip of the tongue. I end up channeling a lot of mothers, grandmothers, and great-grandmothers who communicate their recipe specialties this way. Oftentimes, my client not only recalls the special dish but also has, in their possession at home, the handwritten recipe passed down in the family. I have tasted cakes, pies, preserves, jams and jellies, soups, and stews in addition to a few foreign dishes I could not identify by name but I could describe the ingredients! One was a Brazilian dish made with spicy rice wrapped in banana leaves. I was pleasantly surprised when my client confirmed it. Recently, one grandmother was being very particular in showing me how she was whisking the mixture of the meringue for the lemon meringue pie that was making my mouth pucker.

A lot of times, these same mothers and grandmothers will be mixing up a great-smelling cake while simultaneously communicating, "Happy Birthday!" That tells me that either my client, or another family member, has had a birthday celebration that either just passed (within a month or less) or is pending (again, within a month or less). Sometimes the cake is very specific, such as the one with pink icing or perhaps a coconut cake—all of which is usually relevant. It is truly heartwarming how often such deceased loved ones let clients know that they are not forgotten by acknowledging their birthdays. In the worst-case scenario, I have tasted blood in my mouth and my client will say, "Yes, he put the barrel of a gun in his mouth and pulled the trigger." Again, the taste is fleeting and so any unpleasantness is temporary, and I accept it as part and parcel of the job.

Hopefully this review of the clairs has been useful and validating. You may experience one, two or more of these experiences. You'd be surprised at how many aspiring and practicing psychics are unfamiliar with this information. It should be helpful to identify and pinpoint these sources of information as it pertains to you personally, and the manner in which you are most likely to receive input from Spirit while you are assisting others. You are probably going to receive the information based on your own life experiences, so you can relate to, and identify, the communication readily.

For me, it is always intriguing how the information being received has more than one meaning, and you should be aware of this potential as well. Like hearing a whistle, connected to a client's father, that I associated with the railroad and having her tell me it was actually a toy tin whistle instead. Or on another occasion, I saw the nickname "Carm," which I associated with the name Carmela, but my client told me it was referring to a male relative named Carmine. In these examples, the information was received correctly, just not with the relevance I had assigned to it. And that's the beauty of how Spirit operates.

As you are probably already aware, clients expect you not only to be accurate but to be quick and deliberate about it as well.

No one wants to wait while a psychic hems and haws and beats around the bush. That's sure-fire way to squelch repeat business and good word of mouth. If you are a practicing psychic, even if it's only part-time, weekends or special events, it will be helpful to build a psychic lexicon if you haven't already. A psychic lexicon is a mental catalog of signs and symbols that are all spiritual shorthand for bigger concepts.

The signs and symbols communicate the meaning in a very quick and easy-to-understand way so that you may discern them immediately and can keep things moving along. The signs and symbols are repeated on a regular basis and are not necessarily client-specific, but are generic enough to apply to any number of individuals. Because they turn up so regularly, they have become standard to your practice and are familiar to your usage. The best part, however, is that my lexicon will be unique and different from your lexicon because the information is being filtered through a channel that is uniquely yours alone.

Here are a few sample examples from my lexicon, of which there are presently roughly three dozen. When someone in Spirit throws their hands back simultaneously as if to say, "Hands off," it means that they can offer their insight but otherwise cannot interfere with anyone's free will. A salute is a pretty obvious indication that someone had been in military service. A truck backed into a ditch, its rear tires spinning in mud unable to gain traction, tells me that someone is feeling stuck or stagnant. Striking the center of the chest with an open palm translates to heart attack, heart-related health issues, or anxiety that feels like a heart attack. The length of someone's bare inner arm tells me of addiction for a substance stronger than marijuana. The horizontal length of someone's outstretched arm with the palm up showing "arm's length," tells me there is a geographic or an emotional distance in a relationship.

As you build your lexicon, you may discover that new symbols get added or altered, and others may go dormant. This is okay and to be expected, especially the longer you are a practicing psychic and trends cycle with the times. For example, the teen idol symbol for a Baby Boomer may be David Cassidy, Davy Jones, or Bobby Sherman (are you even old enough to know who they are?). The teen idol symbol for recent times may be Shawn Mendes, Robert Pattison, or Justin Bieber. The same goes for cars, music references, clothing fashions, and so on—anything that would need to adjust in order to keep current with changing tastes and trends in pop culture and technology.

In keeping with the preceding, it will certainly be useful if, in addition to building your personal psychic lexicon, you also try to develop as many new points of reference as possible. Remember, Spirit can only communicate to you the impressions that fall within your own frame of reference. In this way, you will know to identify what's coming through because you've seen it, experienced it, or lived through it. If world geography isn't your strong suit, Spirit won't hold the ability to be as concise as showing you the location of Greece on a mental globe of the world. Instead, you might receive a succession of images associated with Greece such as togas, Greek architecture such as ancient temples, Greek mythology in movies like *Clash of the Titans*, and so on. If you are lacking in certain areas, it will significantly aid you to become more proficient if you expand your knowledge base with as many diverse points of reference as possible. As a helpful hint, a quick, easy, and oftentimes intriguing way of brushing up on a wide variety of such points is by watching TV programs such as *Antiques Roadshow* or *American Pickers* in order to gain lots of historical background and trivia.

You'll also need to determine if Spirit is communicating the information commonly found in your lexicon in a consistent manner. Whenever I receive indication of a calendar month, I am only ever shown the name of the month. This never varies for me in the way that it may for other psychics. So, if I am to communicate the month of July, I will be shown the word "July." You may also be shown the word July, but it may be possible for you to be shown the number "7" indicating the seventh month; or you may be shown a ruby, which is the July birthstone; or you may be shown Cancer the Crab, which is the zodiac symbol for July. You'll want to discern if, for you, there are variable ways to interpret the same meaning, and become acclimated to working this way if so.

In my opinion, and in my experience, the most important areas for developing a strong working knowledge are physical health ailments that can impair the body, causing pain, deterioration, and possible death; and mental health issues that may lead to suicide or addiction. These areas are likely to surface, one way or another, in virtually every psychic reading. Becoming fluent in the function of the body's organs; the circulatory system; potential genetic issues such as diabetes, arthritis, or high blood pressure; and issues particular to men and women's health will be beneficial.

Equally beneficial will be your ability to discuss symptoms of common mental health experiences such as anxiety, depression, bipolar disorder, and personality disorders. This will prevent you from suggesting that a presiding problem with which your client, or her loved ones, is grappling with is merely "behavioral." In this manner, you can advise on courses of action by recommending medical screenings, psychological therapy or psychiatric consultation, and natural healing alternatives as treatment options. It is mandatory, however, that you clearly communicate that the information you are providing only constitutes suggestions and not directives. Unless you are also a physician, mental health counselor or social worker, it is not your place, as a psychic, to prescribe specific treatments. You are offering intuitive guidance only.

It may also be helpful to become culturally competent if you are unfamiliar with the mores and customs of the communities to whom you will be marketing your services. For example, if you are stationed near a military base, you may need to become articulate on not just military terminology and protocol but also on the symptoms of post-traumatic stress disorder, which is experienced by (but often still undiscussed) many military personnel. If you live near a Native-American reservation, familiarize yourself with tribe culture and Native-American spiritual beliefs. Same for residing near, or marketing to, any other minority community—you will gain credibility and integrity among your client population if you can speak knowledgeably about the inner workings of the culture. As such, it has been something of a wake-up call for me to channel clients' deceased loved ones who are of Italian ancestry only to learn that it was commonplace for men to have mistresses and second (sometimes illegitimate) families. I've actually had clients, Italian and otherwise, follow up with me to report that they've discovered siblings or relatives they never knew they had! And there's no need to worry about channeling someone from "The Old Country" who speaks a different language than you do; it will all be filtered through the Spirit equivalent of Google Translate, so your interpretation should be reasonably effortless.

An example of this is the time I was in a psychic session via Skype with a man in India. I know nothing about Indian culture, but I immediately began to channel his grandmother in Spirit. She was small but mighty, wore a red and gold costume, had a gap between her two front teeth, and raised chickens—all of which he verified. She was, of course, speaking in her native tongue, which wasn't an issue to translate, but where we got held up was his inability to understand what she was telling him. He was laid off work and worrying about his future; she, in turn, was encouraging him to use this time to assess his gifts and talents; to develop the ideas he had for technology; and to reconnect with his spirituality. She kept referring him to the name "Ganesh." This came up several times, and each time he said he didn't know who or what that was. It was shown to me one more time, and I insisted he give it careful consideration. Turns out, Ganesh is an Indian god! I was able to tell him Ganesh represented wisdom and prosperity (all true), which is exactly what he needed to hear.

As you become increasingly authentic and adept, it will be tempting to entertain family, friends or neighbors with your heightened psychic abilities and your proficiency for channeling. A word of advice from one who is seasoned in the field: don't do it. Just as many surgeons refuse to operate on their own family members, I strongly suggest you withdraw from making such overtures and that you graciously decline all requests from people well known to you, including loved ones. As much as I like to have fun with clients by injecting some levity when and where appropriate, this is serious stuff, and we shouldn't lose sight of that. If you are truly authentic in who you are and what you do, you are obligated to say what you see. This also means you have no way of foretelling what you see—good, bad, and indifferent.

Reading for people close to you is an accident waiting to happen for a couple reasons. First, you already know way too much about them, so you aren't really "reading" them as much as you are informing or opining based on what you already know to be true. There's no challenge or authenticity in that. Next, you must also remember that in all you do, you could always be wrong. What you are sensing—even if you believe you are channeling Spirit—could always be subject to complete misinterpretation. Are you really going to spills the beans or break bad news without censoring the information? If you are censoring information, are you truly authentic? Should you take this route, be prepared for pushback, hurt feelings, or the dissolution of the relationship entirely.

I am speaking from experience as I lost a couple of friends whom I think were too polite to tell me I was wrong or overcompensating early on in my career. They "ghosted" me, which was heartbreaking, and I never did find out what happened. Similarly, when a neighbor's son asked for a reading, with his father present (who was my neighbor at the time), I tactfully declined by saying, "I don't think that's a good idea. I have to live next door to your parents." What I intended was that, if the reading went south for some reason, the relationship I had built with my neighbors could grow terribly awkward and resentful. You are, of course, free to conduct yourself as you wish in such circumstances but you can see how easily reading for people close to you may create a conflict of interest.

Similarly, please do not approach total strangers on the street, in the grocery store or at the airport, and begin assaulting them with psychic information you are intuiting for them. Real life is not reality TV; and reality TV shows featuring psychics who do this very thing are projecting an extraordinary disservice to those of us who wish to conduct ourselves with integrity. I can assure you that what appears spontaneous on television has all be prearranged and scouted out well in advance, with release forms signed and camera crews set up. I'm not suggesting that the psychic is disingenuous; what I am saying, though, is this type of scenario absolutely sends the wrong message to budding and aspiring psychics by granting license to do the same in real time. Do not emulate this example. Not everyone wants it, is open to it, or welcomes the disruption. It is a highly intrusive thing to do and, if you opt to do it, you darn well better be certain of what you're about to communicate to a stranger who may be suffering or grieving a loss. There have been perhaps one or two instances in which I felt truly compelled to do this, and since those times I have resisted the temptation to do it altogether.

My procedure for conducting a private one-on-one session is to arrive early to bless the space in which I will be working in the manner I have previously described. I then spend the rest of the time in prayer and meditation. Once my client is seated, I explain what he or she may expect of the process to generate a comfort level and put my client at ease. Finally, I say a blessing before turning things over to my Spirit Guides, who are also the gatekeepers for deceased loved ones in Spirit who are connected to my client and who may opt to come forward. The first half of the session, I work intuitively and the second half I offer to the client as an opportunity to ask questions. I also request that each client bring hardcopy photographs of loved ones living or deceased to aid me in attempting to connect with someone by special request, if they are deceased, and to provide keener guidance if they are still living. This is my format, and you may choose to do something similar or format your sessions entirely differently.

How often are you willing to offer readings to the same people? What is the duration of your session? Are you willing and able to offer one-hour, half-hour, or fifteen-minute sessions designated by correlating price points? If so, your flexibility may make your offerings more attractive to a broader number of people. I used to offer half-hour readings but found that, personally speaking, it simply doesn't provide the forum for an in-depth session. I have, though, always had as my professional policy the rule that any client may only book a one-hour, one-on-one appointment with me but once a year. And I must tell you, despite repeated begging and pleading, I have held firm to this position. There are a couple of reasons for my rationale.

First, I do not wish to foster a dependency of any sort. There are many folks who are quite vulnerable mentally-emotionally, and are susceptible to any morsel of optimistic hope or encouragement you can provide. That's fine but a lot of those same individuals may come to look upon what you're offering as cheap therapy or a more accessible replacement for treatment under the guidance of a qualified professional. From a spiritual perspective, I want my clients to have faith in *their* faith. This has often been reinforced by their deceased loved ones who have plainly stated to them, "You don't need this man to connect to me." What this translates to mean is that Spirit is also encouraging my clients' independence, as opposed to dependency on me as the facilitator. There are any number of ways in which my clients (and yours) can connect with their loved ones outside of a psychic session: making an old family recipe; holding a cherished object belonging to the deceased; playing music associated in memory with someone; or simply praying and talking to them.

The second reason why I allow only one reading per year, is that it gives people the opportunity to process the information and reflect upon it at their leisure. I also suggest that each client bring a device with which to record his or her psychic reading. In recent times, people use a memo app or some other comparable download on their cell phone. It is easy and convenient although, through no fault of anyone's, I have discovered that oftentimes the recording doesn't "take" at all, or it cuts out at some point during the session. A recording is good backup, though, as it is not uncommon for people to have lapses in their ability to, again, recall sometimes highly random details that are being relayed during their session.

Every week, I am contacted by clients on my Facebook page who were unable to verify such information in person with me but, upon listening to their playback, have had their memory triggered such that they experienced an Aha! moment. So, the recording was useful in that respect. Also, one reading a year allows the opportunity for any predictions I may have made to come to fruition and play out in due time. More than one client was absolute in denying that no family member was expecting, only to follow up with me upon their annual return that, indeed, a pregnancy was announced shortly after our session. (As a reminder, another benefit of the recording is that, on rare occasion, a "third voice" has been heard, contributing to our conversation, which was unheard at the time of the original reading!)

In keeping with this chapter's theme of "do what you are," you will do well in the longevity of your craft if you distinguish yourself as a breed apart. I don't mean mimic some famous psychic, or create a "gimmick" per se. As you may be discovering for yourself, there are an increasing number of people who are practicing psychics, or aspire to be. Give considerate thought to how you might stand out in the crowd by offering something different and unique. This will make an exchange with you especially memorable, and will generate good word of mouth. For example, early on in my career, I would receive so many visuals in my head when sitting with a client that I would sketch—literally draw on paper—whatever I was "seeing." This made for a nice souvenir and "take away" for each client, and gave prospective clients something to look forward to for having an original work of art, so to speak, crafted just for him or her. Additionally, as an option for my clients I currently offer to conduct a "health scan." While they are seated, I will close my eyes and scan their body from head to toe, and offer feedback about anything of potential concern in the spirit of prevention. This has worked well and, in several instances, I caught thyroid cancer, diabetes, and breast cancer in people who didn't realize it. Someone whom I have mentored, and who I have encouraged to strike out on her own, decided to hold small gatherings of people and "read" personal objects each person brought with them (this is known as psychometry). This is certainly an original take on a group-reading scenario, and I applaud her ingenuity.

My most favorite facet of my work is conducting group gatherings or galleries, similar to the preceding example by my friend. You may have seen television segments that demonstrate psychic galleries in which a number of people come together, and the psychic stands before them while providing intuitive information or even channels deceased loved ones. I have conducted gallery events for as few as ten people and for as many as nearly 300. I enjoy the spontaneity of the experience and I find that oftentimes people who do not get singled out still leave feeling enlightened. If you choose to hold a psychic gallery, the structure and format will be up to you to determine in advance. Will you give each person in attendance some one-on-one time? Will you be in psychic-only mode, providing intuitive information to your group about aspects of their lives? Or are you confident enough to serve as a medium, and channel Spirit in such a setting? If so, how will you do this? Will you have group members make requests? Also, will you allow for questions or will it be entirely whatever you feel compelled to provide? These are all points to ponder before holding such an event.

For me, personally, when I hold a psychic gallery, it is formatted into two sections. The first hour, I work with the audience by channeling Spirit after which we take an intermission (an hour of sitting is taxing on folks, no matter how compelling you may be). After the break, I take special requests via audience questions for another hour. I always arrive an hour in advance to say a blessing in the space in which I will be working before spending the remaining time in prayer and meditation privately. When the event starts, I introduce myself and prepare the group for what to expect and how things will flow, just as I would for a private session. This warm-up time not only sets my audience at ease in getting a "feel" for who I am, it serves the same purpose for me.

Once I explain how the event will transpire, I say a separate non-denominational blessing with the folks present before launching into the event. As a way of engaging them further, I also request a timekeeper so I don't have to worry about tracking time on a clock and can focus on the work at hand without distraction. (As a nicety, I try to remember to offer my timekeeper the right of first refusal to ask a question upon return from intermission for being such a good sport and helping me out.) With larger groups, I have a lottery drawing by pulling ticket stubs from a container, keeping things fair in terms of who is randomly selected to ask questions in my second half of an event. This format may work for you too, or you may decide upon doing something entirely different. I especially appreciate the moments when Spirit has me clasp both outstretched arms together at the palms, hold one arm stationary and expand the other arm to span the entire audience. This symbolizes that the bit of wisdom about to be communicated is intended for all to hear, so no one leaves empty handed.

Something unusual has occurred for me over the course of the past several years. As a collector, I often find myself in antique malls and collectibles co-op shops. I discovered that if I went to such a place about 24 to 48 hours in advance of a psychic gallery, I would be provided with a series of clues to inform how I begin the event. I know it sounds crazy but it works every time—it *never* fails! When I pull into the parking lot of an antique mall, I sit in my car and recite the Lord's Prayer. I next indicate that what's about to happen is intended for my event coming up on such-and-such a night. I then go in with my pad of paper and pen, and start to walk the aisles, waiting for my attention to be distracted to very specific, yet highly obscure, items which I then note on my pad of paper. Once I feel that I have enough notes, or I have finished walking the store, I know I have gathered the details that will single out the one person in the room at my upcoming event for whom *all* the criteria will make total sense. My psychic gallery begins with my reciting the list of items to which I was drawn. It usually takes several minutes for folks to connect the dots, and I often repeat my list two or three times, but in the end, just one person alone connects with every piece of it. It is incredibly fascinating! (When I've been unable to get to an antique mall, I can page through a stack of old magazines instead, and the process works the same and just as well.)

If you're having a tough time imaging what this is like, here's an example. Upon entering an antique shop, I was drawn to a small pile of old postcards. The one on top was a valentine addressed to a "Bertha" and dated 1903. As I looked up, across the aisle, was a calendar dated 1903. This told me the early 1900s was Bertha's era, so I made note of this. I was also feeling there was a German or Pennsylvania Dutch association, and I kept seeing items connected to farming including cloth feed sacks, equipment, and a toy farm. I also noted old, rusty railroad spikes that I felt tied to Reading, Pennsylvania and the Reading Railroad. Finally, I was seeing prints, photos, and figurines that led me to believe that Bertha had two daughters.

When I revealed this data at the psychic gallery, sure enough, only one person claimed all of it. Well, claimed almost all of it. She had ancestors from Reading, PA that were Pennsylvania Dutch with a farm and railroad connection. And what of the two daughters? The great-grandmother she was thinking of actually had *four* daughters, two of which were still alive. Two of great-grandmother's daughters had two daughters, one of which had two daughters—one of whom was the very person with whom I was interacting. The only piece absent was affirmation for the name Bertha. However, after making a phone call to her sister, the woman was able to validate that their great-grandmother was indeed named Bertha!

On another specific occasion, I went through my usual routine and upon entering the antique mall, I was "told" to walk in a direction different from the way I ordinarily would have. I saw two dolls from the early 1960s representing Pebbles and Bamm-Bamm from the classic cartoon series *The Flintstones*. I was trying to figure out whether it was a reference to *The Flintstones* or possibly a reference to the name "Fred" after the show's lead protagonist. Nevertheless, I jotted it down on my notepad. I next was drawn to objects related to fishing—fishing rods, old lures, a tackle box, and the image of a fisherman on the cover of an old magazine. I then noticed a Steiff stuffed animal of a Cocker Spaniel, and jotted it down. I also kept seeing coins but, in particular, commemorative coins created to honor special occasions (jotted it down). Finally, I saw a number of Coca-Cola items and made note of these as well. It was with this list of items that I began my event. After a few moments pause, one person in a group of over 40 raised her hand and said she thought these were all references to her deceased father.

She explained that her dad lived in Alaska and was an avid fisherman, known for his smoked salmon. When she was sixteen, he gave her a black Cocker Spaniel puppy and she went on to breed them for many years. Her father collected coins and left behind a collector's edition box of state quarters to be given to each of her children upon their graduation from school. And he was an antiques enthusiast with a special interest in Coca-Cola! In fact, hanging on her wall was one of several Coke crates he had given her. Once she confirmed my list of antique-mall observations, I was able to channel her father easily. Somehow, someway, he knew 48 hours in advance that she would be attending the gallery. But what of the *Flintstones* reference? She followed up with an e-mail validation, telling me she often watched *The Flintstones* as a kid and used to think her dad looked like Fred Flintstone! She affirmed that once I mentioned the Cocker Spaniels, she knew for sure. She closed by thanking me again for sharing her dad's messages. (Oddly enough, as I was responding to her message, I received a spam e-mail for an Alaskan vacation!)

In addition to providing psychic readings and perhaps group events, you will make yourself most marketable (and increase the likelihood of generating a sustainable income) if you diversify what you are able to offer. Do you already have a specialty? Perhaps you are skilled in using Tarot cards or angel cards or runes. If so, be certain these modalities are something you genuinely enjoy and not a crutch for lacking in the confidence to put yourself "out there" free from devices of any sort. This is sometimes the case for people who are just starting out in this field. I experienced it myself when I used to wear a bracelet with meaningful and relevant phrases written on it. I used to reflect on it in solitude just prior to beginning a psychic gallery event until one evening, right before I was to start, the bracelet broke and fell from my wrist to the floor. In that moment, I knew that I would no longer need it, and allowed myself to hold greater faith for my personal and spiritual abilities.

In addition to various modalities for offering readings to potential clients, you may also be, or train to be, proficient in reiki and massage. You may have any number of spiritual or even paranormal areas of special interest to you, such that you could develop presentations based on what you've learned or experienced. Topics could cover meditation, crystals, ghost hunting, numerology, astrology, holistic wellness and nutrition— the list is endless and is limited only by your ability to mobilize your efforts and manifest them into being. Perhaps you are able to funnel your knowledge base into mentoring workshops such as I have done. More on all of this will be detailed in the last chapter of this book.

When I was developing my psychic abilities, I didn't have anyone to help me or show me the ropes, so to speak. Being completely self-taught in all I do, I determined that no one with whom I came into contact, and who was seeking this type of information, would go without. I created an experiential, hands-on and daylong workshop by which I walk participants through all that I know. At day's end, I pair them up with total strangers and give each tandem team a number of exercises to do with each other, such as intuiting information about a loved one by looking at their photo, or doing the same holding a loved one's treasured object. Other exercises include gathering information by simply looking at a first name, written on a piece of paper, with whom the exercise partner has a special bond. I have been teaching this workshop since the mid-2000s and never have I been disappointed in how amazingly participants are able to surprise and please themselves while aweing and amazing their exercise partners, and often myself. So popular was this workshop, that I developed a level II version that includes mediumship, automatic writing, and other activities.

The possibilities for carving out a specialized niche for yourself are truly endless. Because you are unique and eclectic, what you have to say, show, and offer will be unlike anything offered by other practitioners. Assess yourself, what attracts you or holds your interest, and then create it. Doing this in concert with a Spirit Guide, or other guiding, spiritual resources, should gain you confidence to debut a range of services, events, and educational, fun, and enlightening workshops and classes. Never be afraid to tell your story, and to reveal your mistakes and vulnerabilities as part of what you intend to communicate. It will endear you to others for humbling yourself as human, and not someone separate and apart from others such that you appear untouchable, inauthentic or both.

Chapter 3

Your Clients and Their Questions

As a practicing psychic, you are probably encountering a diverse range of clientele. Perhaps because I am older and more seasoned (in appearance and experience), I tend to attract folks who are 35 and up. If you are younger, you may attract similar-age peers who think psychics are cool, edgy and hip. Like myself, your clients are probably about 85% women and 15% men, as it seems as though women are more likely to be open and accepting of what we do. It is refreshing, though, to encounter open-minded males and, oftentimes, they have had spiritual awakenings that prompted them to be more willing to explore unlimited (and unexplainable) possibilities. These kinds of men are always a pleasure to read, and make my job effortless.

In one or two instances, I've had a wife or girlfriend "spring" a psychic reading on their male counterpart by not telling him where they were going until they enter the office of wherever I happen to be and meet me for the first time. To be honest, this really rubs me the wrong way and, in my opinion, demonstrates disrespect for how sacred I hold the process. I am not a showbiz "act" to entertain in the manner of a performer. I always ensure that the gentlemen want to go forward with the reading despite having been blindsided. Unless you're okay with a situation this spontaneous, it is not good practice in my book. In the next chapter on skeptics, I will discuss other types of folks, especially males, who are cynical and judgmental.

If you haven't already done so, you'll occasionally receive requests from parents to read their children. Whether you opt to do so or not will be your professional judgment call. Personally, I question why a parent would think this necessary, and I have been adamant in the past that the young person must *want* the session and not feel obligated or pressured into it. If it is not the child initiating the desire for a psychic reading, in that case, I always decline. I would also not feel comfortable reading anyone under the age of 12. (I once had a woman want to bring her toddler to me for a reading!) Reading children is challenging because they don't usually have the kind of ability to recall with clarity in order to validate much of what you're telling them. They are also usually unaware of details about their ancestors or don't particularly have a strong connection to anyone who has passed on for being so young. It can be rather frustrating in an attempt to fill a full session if the child is only able to speak in generalities, or provides ambiguous responses, or doesn't really have a grasp of the process. As such, you're likely to receive a lot of "I don't knows" in response. Assess how to make this judgment call about children based on your own intuition and the maturity level of the individual.

On the plus side, some kids are almost painfully sensitive, and may find relief at the chance to talk to someone older and wiser who's "been there, done that" to offer them reassurances, especially if they're frightened and anxious about what's happening to them. In hindsight, I think I would have welcomed the steady and compassionate reassurance of an adult who could have waylaid my adolescent concerns. Young folks can have very strong communicative connections to animals and this may be something of which to encourage development. Sensitive kids oftentimes feel like social outcasts and loners, so perhaps you can facilitate a discussion group or workshop geared toward such kids if you know of enough of them who wish to gather in a safe forum. Children are also much closer, and more accustomed, to having been in soul form than in human form. As such, they may provide insights into Heaven and the afterlife; they may offer previously unconsidered perspectives and truths for being so frank and candid; and they may have a salient knowledge of their own past lives to make for a fascinating discussion.

You may be called upon to use your intuition to discern if what you have to offer is a good match for a prospective type of client. As I mentioned, I allow people to see me one time a year. When people press me to make an exception because they are feeling desperate, it makes me very uncomfortable because they are asking that I breach my ethical code for them, and that feels greedy regardless of their situation. Bottom line is, *there is no such thing as a psychic emergency*. If someone's situation is that desperate, a psychic is the *last* person they should be contacting in lieu of calling 911, Child Protective Services, or other community social and emergency service organizations. If they remain dissatisfied with my edict, they are certainly free to find someone else who does what I do; there's plenty of folks out there. But I question the mindset of reaching out to me versus couples counseling, Alcoholics or Narcotics Anonymous, and so on. Of course, if you choose to make exceptions where I do not, be prepared for word to spread, and that might cause backlash if you have been inconsistent in your own policies and procedures.

As I also alluded to earlier, you run the potential to be attracting people who are mentally-emotionally fragile, who do not have a formal mental health diagnosis (or are in denial of it), and are not consistently using prescription medication or are self-medicating with other substances. They may see you as a cheaper, more mystical alternative to consultation with a clinician or mental health counselor. This is why some psychological background and some awareness of mental illness symptomology could prove useful. But tread delicately. If someone is truly fragile and needy, you certainly don't want to risk making them, or their situation, worse.

There have been many occasions for which I have preceded a statement by qualifying clearly that I am not a marriage counselor, abuse counselor, psychiatrist, and so on. I have had situations in which I have very gently guided someone to see the possibility that what they're experiencing is not their fault because they come by it honestly. This means that because of their family history, which I have intuited, there's a "trickle-down" effect; that is, there is a genetic predisposition for depression, anxiety, bipolar disorder and so on based on the client's heredity. They may be relieved to be granted this more global perspective, as it may answer lifelong questions by placing interlocking puzzle pieces into place at long last. The client may also be relieved to know that what they've been experiencing has a name. So empowered, they may break an old pattern and a vicious cycle of blaming themselves with self-deprecating thoughts of inferiority. If you are not comfortable in broaching such discussions (and you will likely need to at some future point), you may wish to speak in terms of generalities, using phrasing such as "a case of the blues," or referencing someone's impulsivity or unrealistic ideas. This may also pertain to discussing a client's loved ones, children, and spouse or partner.

If you are able to compassionately lead such a discussion by illuminating the truth, slowly but surely, it could lead to a personal awakening for the client. When I have done this, I have followed it up by discussing possible options, balancing traditional

Western approaches such as psychiatry, psychology and pharmaceuticals with a discussion about holistic options such as lifestyle and relationship adjustments, natural supplements and remedies, and revisions to a diet and exercise program. Perhaps, depending upon the client, a blending of both approaches will fit for them; but, ultimately, the choice is theirs to make, and you must be very deliberate in saying as much so your client understands that he or she is responsible for their own choices.

Sometimes people become so desperate that they stretch what you are saying to fit something completely unrelated, like forcing a square peg into a round hole. They so want to believe that you will fulfill their hopes that they also delude themselves into believing that what you're communicating is relevant when it is not. This most often occurs when clients come in with a very specific agenda, which I always discourage. When I sense this, I gently request that they set aside their preconceived notions in order to allow me to guide the session. I tell them, "It's going to be what's it's going to be, and I can't make it be something it's not. Please just follow my lead and validate what you're able to." Once when I was describing details connected to a client's grandmother, I mentioned seeing Easter eggs. Breathless and gasping for air, she said, "Yes, yes! She made meatballs all the time!" Huh? The two have nothing in common, but she was, perhaps, drawing conclusions based on the size of Easter eggs and meatballs (and I'm only guessing that's what it was). In another instance, I asked a client about a male who had passed with a "J" name and, eyes brimming with tears, she said, "My husband Steve!" Huh? Again, this was an example of desperation clouding someone's commonsense.

In keeping with this thought, I sometimes have to remind clients that I should not only be guiding the discussion, I should be doing most of the talking during it. In striving to be as authentic as can be, I want to know as little about each client as possible. In fact, I only get their first name in advance of an appointment. But some folks simply do not grasp the concept or, as I stated previously, see our psychic session as grief or mental health counseling. When this happens, they start spilling *everything* in great detail. There have been occasions when I have stopped the session to politely, but firmly, tell them that they are sabotaging their own reading by divulging way too much information. Usually saying that helps (although some folks with the "gift of gab" have a difficult time exercising restraint). There have been times, however, when they still don't hear me, and I sit back and allow them to vent and ramble on because it seems as though that is what's necessary for them in the moment. And, truthfully, perhaps they have had mystical or spiritual experiences that they can only share with someone they feel will understand and believe them.

What kinds of questions do most people want to know? Again, this will depend on how you market yourself, whether it is as a psychic or a psychic medium. If the latter, rest assured that expectations are high that you will be able to bring forth a cherished loved one in Spirit. Otherwise, typical questions concern health (and that of family members); financial future; travel; relocation (as in moving or moving out of state); changing jobs; and...drum roll, please...*romance*! Wanting to know about the future with a current relationship or finding Mr. Right (and remember, the majority of your clientele is likely to be female) is the most pressing question that most clients will usually want to know about. This extends to pinning down his first name, how they will meet, the time of year to expect this to occur—it sometimes even extends to, "Will I have children with this man?" If you are solid in making predictions, and you are finely attuned to all things feminine, this type of reading may be right up your alley.

In keeping with the preceding, I am reminded of the time I briefly worked for one of those psychic hotlines that you used to see advertised on television. There are any number of them, and there is an audition-screening process by which you (usually) need to read two different individuals who then submit their feedback to the person who hires. I originally applied for "the" leading, premier psychic hotline and aced both of the screenings; some of the feedback I received said, "He's probably the most accurate psychic I've read with thus far. I never had to ask a question because he had touched on all the major areas of my life. He was very spiritual, nice and funny. He talked about my past with so much detail that he blew my mind." But I found the business's online reporting portals difficult to navigate and decided it was too much effort for too little income, so I opted out. I did apply to another psychic hotline, aced the two screenings, and worked for them for three months. What I discovered was that the vast majority of callers were women and what 90% of them wanted to know was if their boyfriend was ever going to leave his wife for them! As you can imagine, this was dissatisfying to me and after giving it a fair shake, I left there as well (although I have remained friends with the person who hired me).

Over the years, some of the queries clients have made of me have led me to believe I was being interviewed or screened by them, as if to ascertain that I meet their standards. The questions that rather ruffle my feathers are, "What's your religion?" and "Are you a Christian?" Of course, neither I nor you are obligated to respond to such questions; it's no one's business and, for me, it has no personal or professional bearing on how I interact with my clients. I suppose I can appreciate where some folks are coming from when they ask this of me. If it doesn't feel like they're being nosey or judgmental they may just be making an effort to reconcile what I do with their own religious upbringing. It may be that, for their own peace of mind, they want to feel "safe" and not as if they are breaching the religious tenets with which they were raised (more on this subject in the next chapter on skeptics). If you are made to feel put in an awkward position should someone ask these or other personal and religious questions about how you conduct yourself or your business, you are free to respond (or not) however you feel comfortable.

Another line of questions that irks me immediately conveys to me that the person making the inquiry either doesn't understand what I do or is sarcastically mocking what I do. It doesn't occur very often (in fact, I think I could count on one hand the number of occasions it has), but when it does, the person asking gets schooled! Those questions are of the "get-rich-quick" or personal gain line of questioning such as "Who's going to win the Super Bowl?" or even worse, "What are my winning lottery numbers?" I don't know about you, but if you strive for authenticity as I do, your response will be to shut these types of questions down rapidly. First of all, I am virtually sports-illiterate and could care less who's playing in the Super Bowl let alone who's going to win—it's not my thing, and it's not what I do. Second, even if I *could* give out winning lottery numbers, I certainly never would! Again, it's not who I am or what I'm about. Personally, I think winning the lottery would be the *worst* thing that could happen and would create more headaches than it would solve problems, no matter how altruistic folks claim they'd be with their winnings. I'd rather see people invest the spare dollars they spend on lottery tickets doing something that will better serve others. Period.

There's another question that I receive from time to time that seems to be in keeping with people's comfort level about their religious beliefs and seeking consultation with a psychic, and that is, "Is there a hell?" I sometimes think this may be motivated by my client having known someone who was a bad person, or having known someone who has taken his or her own life. I can only respond by telling them what I have been shown in dreams and meditations, or what I have seen in my work channeling other people's loved ones. And that is, "No, there is no hell per se. The only 'hell' that exists is in our own mind." I'll get into this more in-depth in the chapter on ghosts but, suffice it to say, if you believe you are going to hell when you die, then your own fears, anxieties, or inability to atone for your gross acts of misconduct, may cause you to become "stuck." I firmly believe that no one is turned away from entering Heaven, no one is condemned, punished, or rejected *but* you have to *want* to be there. And being there requires someone to take responsibility for their bad acts by confronting the truth, which is something that may be a prolonged process for some more than others.

It's surprising to me—and a bit sad—to acknowledge that a commonly asked question I receive is, "Is my loved one safe and at peace?" My answer has always been consistently the same as it is simplistic in its wisdom: "You don't need me to tell you that. Your faith should tell you that. Listen to what your heart tells you; therein lies the answer." I'm not sure what would prompt a client to ask such a thing; when I channel a loved one, oftentimes they'll still ask, "Is he in Heaven?" My response is, "Yes, otherwise I wouldn't be talking to him so readily and effortlessly." There always seems to be such a great relief expressed at hearing this. Perhaps it is one of those situations in which the deceased person led a questionable lifestyle and those who remain behind have cause to wonder if he or she made it safely to the other side. There have been a couple of instances in which I find myself communicating with someone who resisted leaving and was existing as a ghost; but, again, more on that later.

Along the same line of questioning, clients will sometimes ask me to convey something to a deceased loved one on their behalf. It is nearly heartbreaking to have someone say, "Please tell him I love him" or "Please tell him how much I miss him." In other instances, a client might say, "Please tell her I'm sorry...I wasn't there when she passed; was unable to attend the service; or wasn't able to keep a promise connected to the funeral arrangements." On these occasions, I, again, consistently reply,

"You don't need me to tell your loved one that. You can communicate to them on your own and say exactly what you just did. They will hear you and feel your emotion, guaranteed." This is about empowering people to take stock of their own faith while minimizing dependency on an outside third party, meaning you or I in this type of situation.

On a semi-regular basis, clients have also asked me a very challenging and sensitive question. I have had people who have very much wanted to hear from the son or daughter who died at childbirth, was still-born, or died in infancy from Sudden Infant Death Syndrome. I have to confess, I have never been able to do it, and I'm not certain of the reasons for that. Perhaps it's because the soul hadn't full integrated with the physical form, or the personality hadn't developed enough for me to gain an impression. What I have been shown consistently in these instances, however, is that the tragic passing of such a small baby was not without purpose and was, in fact, intended to unite the surviving family to bond and rally and strengthen in their love.

Similarly, I have discovered that I simply stink at helping clients to locate lost or missing objects, although I know that there are psychics who are fantastic at it. I envy them! Periodically, folks have asked me what happened to a missing ring, for example, or where they might find an important document or family photograph left behind by a deceased parent. I'm always willing to try my best on their behalf and I usually come up with at least one possibility. But I've never had anyone follow up with me to victoriously exclaim, "You were right! It was exactly where you said it would be!" If I had requests such as these more frequently, perhaps I could develop my skills in that department.

Do you believe in curses, or that someone can place a curse on you? If so, then you will be cursed! This is one of those no-brainer type of questions that you may be surprised people ask for being anxious and worried. In some cultures, curses are very much ingrained in the cultural belief system and are taken quite seriously. In my opinion and in my experience, no one and nothing can curse someone unless they deeply believe it can happen. Perhaps the person asking is very vulnerable, susceptible or impressionable to the power of suggestion. Or perhaps they are grappling with a mental health issue. I recall once doing a reading (or attempting to do so) for a woman who slowly revealed that she was, at the least, overwhelmed with paranoia if not full-on bipolar disorder.

She claimed that her neighbors were all witches who had cast spells on her. She said they enter her house when she goes out and place voodoo hexes all about. She claimed they even followed her wherever she went, and that she could turn around in any given store and there one of them would be. In trying to rationalize with her (and also realistically undermine her contentions), I told her if she was being surveilled so closely, or felt she was in danger, that she should go to the police. "I can't," she claimed, "they're all in on it!" So vast was the network of witches, she said, that they had a grip on her entire town, so intent were they on monitoring her every move. "What does your husband say about all this?" I asked. "He doesn't believe me either," she complained, which I found quite telling. I tried referring her for counseling, just for the opportunity to have someone else to listen to her and talk her through some options, but I don't think she heard me. Besides, if the "witches" all melted away, she'd no longer be the center of attention—and that might be more threatening to her than her own fabricated delusions.

Another area I refuse to address is making predictions about death and dying, and I recommend you follow suit. It may sound inconceivable, but there are people who have asked me, "When will my mother...husband...grandfather die?" (In one instance, a client asked me to tell her not only when she would die but *how*—can you imagine!) In response, I flatly state, "I'm sorry but you're asking the wrong person. That's not something that I do." Sometimes I am asked about others' deaths, it feels motivated by vindictiveness or greed, and that's an uncomfortable position to be put in. In some instances, it may be that folks are suffering caregiver burnout, and simply want to know when it will all be over, particularly if their loved one has dementia or is in pain and discomfort or is virtually comatose and on life support. While I may empathize with their predicament, it is not my place, nor would I ever want, to predict someone's death. I don't want the heaviness or gravity of that kind of responsibility; and I certainly do not wish to interfere with the divine plan of anyone's individual soul. People can surprise us with spontaneous remissions, recoveries, and moments of lucid clarity. As a matter of ethics, I advise that you decline to answer these kinds of questions, as do I.

Occasionally, clients will ask me about past lives. Ordinarily this is something I perceive rather spontaneously. You may find this is an area of personal interest and expertise and, if so, more power to you! It is a fascinating facet of our field, and has been shown to both help and heal people where traditional medical or psychological interventions have been ineffective. Oftentimes, glimpsing into someone's past life or lives provides explanations for longstanding issues that have remained outstanding and unresolved for decades in some cases. Sometimes, clients have long been haunted by snippets of such visions in recurring dreams that simply won't cease. I have seen instances in which the reason why a client has been unable to let go of an old boyfriend or ex-husband is because she was his mother in a past life!

In one example, the client was a prostitute in the 1800s who selfishly abandoned her son; hearing this caused my client to weep as it "felt" so familiar to her. In several other examples of the same abandonment scenario, I've seen that my clients died during childbirth, bleeding out, and feeling angst, guilt, or obligation for the soul that was the newborn infant and is now the incorrigible boyfriend. And there have been one or two times for which similar maternal callings have extended to the mother who lost her only son to combat in the second World War or in Vietnam. In each case, there was "bleed-over" or seepage from the past-life scenario that extended into the present life. If it truly resonates with the client, presenting the past life portrait not only explains a lot, it creates a sense of calm and inner peace. And the recurring nightmares often stop as well. I usually qualify discussion of past lives by saying that we don't know with absolute certainty if the scenario is completely authentic; but, even so, it serves as a spiritual parable that still resonates nonetheless.

On rare occasion, I see that the past life experienced by a client wasn't as a human being at all, if you can imagine it! The soul may take many forms and that doesn't always pertain to incarnating as human; there are countless ways of being in the Universe. The strange thing is, I've never had a client say, "That's really ridiculous" or "That makes absolutely no sense to me." In each instance, it has resonated with them uniquely and individually. For example, when reading for one client, I was reminded of a very vivid dream of my own in which I suddenly realized I was able to facilely breathe underwater. When I relayed to my client that I believed she may have belonged to a race of aquatic beings, she replied that it made total sense as she has always been drawn to the water, and has always felt comfortable in water, more so than on solid ground.

In about half a dozen cases, I have slowly and gently revealed to my clients—this time usually males—that it appeared as though they had previously led lives as extraterrestrials, believe it or not. Each time, they have burst into tears upon hearing this news. Oddly enough, they all tend to look just as you might expect them to, with long, narrow faces; large, dark eyes; two dots for nostrils; and a thin, lipless mouth. They have typically spent their entire lives feeling socially ostracized as outliers. They do not

71

understand selfishness and greed. They have been quiet, gentle to the point of passivity, and very much focused on helping others to the best of their abilities. They are almost always misunderstood and misinterpreted by others. And they care deeply for the preservation of our natural resources and wildlife. Fascinating, isn't it!

Speaking of wildlife, I am sometimes asked if we reincarnate as animals or if loved ones come back as animals. My impression is, no, we do not reincarnate as animals. But I cannot state that definitively as I do not portend to have all the answers and to be all-knowing. However, it simply doesn't make good sense to me that if someone has evolved and progressed to the point of being a human being, reversing that evolution to return as a cat, a horse, a bird or some other creature would be efficacious to the soul. There may be exceptions, of course, such as a human soul choosing to learn about loyalty in canine form, or electing to understand humility as an abused animal. I also don't believe that when we see a living creature which we might identify with a deceased loved one, such as a brilliant red cardinal or the Monarch butterfly, that it *is* the reincarnation of the loved one. This creates a lot of confusion in our field.

What I do think is possible is that a deceased loved one's soul energy could impress itself upon a living creature so that it randomly manifests to create an affirmation in the moment it is needed. It may be because someone is deeply grieving or because someone is reliving a pleasant memory. This is the manner in which such appearances usually come to fruition, and it is indeed a lovely and pleasing thing that appears coincidental on the surface. I have, myself, experienced it when thinking of a young man I never knew in person but whom I aided to cross over when he was trying to hold on as a ghost. I was on a walk, wondering if he had been in Heaven long enough to understand how to collaborate with living creatures in the way I just described. In the next beat, I turned my head and looked, and there, staring right at me, was a lone fawn. Its mother was nowhere to be seen—which is highly unusual—and it didn't seem threatened or intimidated by my presence. We just locked eyes for a couple minutes, before I smiled and walked away. It was a memorable moment indeed.

It hasn't happened too often in my experience but you may find that, on occasion, a client doesn't want to know personal information about themselves. Instead, they are interested in receiving intuitive information about world events or even celebrities in politics and royalty, sports and entertainment. One client had a lifelong crush on a television soap opera actor and, handing me his 8 x 10" glossy head shot, asked if she would ever have a relationship with him. If this is outside your wheelhouse, as it is for me, you can decline to respond merely by asserting that it's not something you do unless it's an area of special interest for you. You may already be sensitively attuned to global happenings, perhaps even before they occur. If you have a track record with premonitions for natural disasters, epidemics, wars, politics, and current events, you could incorporate that into how you promote yourself if you think it would stimulate client interest.

Oftentimes, the people asking about celebrities want predictions about a certain famous figure's future—will they marry, separate, or divorce? Will they have a baby? And so on. There have been some psychics that have built careers doing this for various tabloid publications and other outlets. A new trend on YouTube has been psychics who "channel" deceased celebrities. Honestly, this feels a bit too attention-seeking for my tastes, especially if the celebrity is recently deceased or died in a controversial manner. It is entirely your choice if you decide to pursue this line of questioning, but know that the ability to be fact-checked is as easy as a computer mouse click. So, it's important to be both accurate and authentic otherwise you risk word-of-mouth damage to your reputation and credibility.

The questions I most enjoy receiving from clients are those that ask me about my own abilities. I appreciate these kinds of questions because it indicates a willingness to understand how someone like you and I can do what we do. Typical queries of this nature include, "Did you always know you could do this?" "Doesn't it exhaust you?" and "How do you cope when you're out in public? Are you bombarded by things you're picking up?" (For the record, my replies are "No, not until I was in my forties," "Yes, but that's the job," and "No, because I control it, it doesn't control me.") Sometimes when clients ask personal questions about my work and abilities, it is because they want something with which to contrast and compare against their own experiences. Asking about myself helps them to suss out that information so they feel as though they're not alone. It can lead to a good and empowering discussion by which the client may be both relieved and confident. As I always do, you might direct the client to outside resources that would be purposeful in addition to anything else you may wish to offer him or her.

Regardless of the questions you are asked, the language with which you reply is most important. I touched on this a bit earlier in this chapter when discussing the importance of delicately framing the topic of psychological and mental health issues so as not to harm or offend. The words we choose are crucial and language matters. I am very conscious of what I say and I choose my words carefully before I say them. One of the reasons why I suggest clients record their sessions with me is that they may not be in a position to absorb all that I am telling them, especially if the information is hard to hear and challenging to assimilate. Listening back to a recording in which my phrasing is very deliberate protects my integrity against false accusations of a client claiming I told them something I did not. It may also grant them a renewed perspective once they've had a chance to clear the barrage of thoughts and feelings, and listen back with a level head.

Therefore, it is important that when you speak with clients in terms of future predictions, that you speak in terms of possibilities versus using definitive language. I'm not suggesting that you should speak in such broad terms as to be vague and ambiguous; otherwise, your client will feel cheated and you will feel lacking in authenticity. But it is imperative that you stress that what you are predicating is *one* possible scenario or that it *may* occur. I suggest you use "maybe" instead of "will"; "could" in place of "definitely"; and "perhaps" instead of "absolutely." This creates some wiggle room for your misinterpretation of what you are perceiving because, after all, you could always be wrong. This reinforces my contention that you should never go down the path of making predictions about anyone's death. It is not our place to do so and, as I said, you risk discrediting yourself (and stigmatizing other psychics by association) for being painfully inaccurate.

If you are uncertain about what you're getting, it is okay to ask clarifying questions. I used to be strongly opposed to doing this as I felt that I should have the ability to be accurate enough to be more direct and concise. But I've acquiesced in my old age. There's a difference between fishing for information with a generic question such as, "Does the color yellow mean anything to you?" as opposed to asking something much more pointed as in, "Do you recall having a yellow cashmere sweater given to you by your grandmother?" That's a big difference. In both examples, the hypothetical psychic should be asking the question because of an impression he or she is receiving that requires clarification. The distinction is that the former question suggests someone not yet as skilled or adept as they could be; the latter question suggests someone getting very specific information and needing verification.

As such, your readings should be a balanced combination of pointed questions backed up with declarative statements. Here's a real-life sample of how this might play out:

Me (to client whose deceased brother I am channeling): "Have you seen a *whale*?"

Client: "Yeah, like five days ago!"

Me: "Because your brother is telling me he influenced that creature to appear at a time that you would see it. Was there anyone else who saw it?"

Client: "Yeah, my sister was with me."

Me: "It was his 'hello' to you both."

I later learned that the whale is symbolic of wisdom, good luck, and long-lasting love—all relevant to my client and his situation. Working toward this question/statement approach will behoove you as you continue to evolve and hone your craft. No one will be able to fault you for asking a very specific question that really nails it by providing a client with affirmation and healing.

Chapter 4

Skeptics

Before we delve into the topic of skeptics and skepticism, let me state at the start that I am, myself, a skeptic. I take what I do quite seriously and I have very high standards for my own levels of authenticity and accuracy. I always strive for 90% or greater in my work, believing that no human being can possibly be 100%. When I think as though I'm closer to 90% than I am to 100%, I feel I haven't delivered the best to my client even though he or she may be satisfied (and perhaps that's because they haven't anything against which to compare except what they've seen on television). As such, I am my own worst critic when judging myself against my own litmus-test standards. An example of this distinction in quality was discussed in the previous chapter in which I made the comparison between asking clients rather vague, seemingly random questions—that type that feel like fishing for information—versus a very pointed and specific question clearly prompted by receiving psychic impressions.

I also have a very sensitive radar to others who work in this field that, in my opinion, fall short of authenticity. It may be because I have an edge for discerning what does or does not ring true. This includes people who have a self-appointed title or made-up name that not only distinguishes them from the layperson, it serves to *elevate* them above the average person by projecting a persona of superiority. This feels entirely disingenuous, particularly if they don't have the goods to back it up. That gives the rest of us a bad name, which hurts the reputations of those of us who aspire to do good works. I'm not sure that these individuals could even be considered legitimate psychics as opposed to opportunists, but more on that shortly.

A skeptic is someone who is questioning, scrutinizing, and discerning—and that's a good thing. Not everything is something, and there are people who become preoccupied with interpreting everything that unfolds around them as a "sign." However, the surprising secret behind a healthy skepticism is that the person— who is attempting to distinguish something truly authentic from that which is fraudulent—is probably using their own gut intuition to do so! As such, skeptics are not total pushovers but are open-minded and willing to change their mindset based on first-hand information. It is in this way that fence-sitting skeptics become believers, who then become *knowers* for having witnessed something that defies logical explanation and can only be labeled as spiritual or even miraculous.

In retrospect, I understand now how fortunate I was to be part of a family that was open-minded. My parents were always of the opinion that humankind was never intended to have all the answers, and there are simply some things in this world that will forever remain mysterious and without scientific explanation. As such, it was commonplace for us to have dinner-table conversation that covered topics such as UFOs, ghosts, Bigfoot, the Loch Ness Monster, and so on. I have learned from talking with other folks my age that this was definitely not the norm! But, then, if you had told me when I was 11 or so that one day I would be working as a psychic medium and writing books, such as this one, on the topic, I wouldn't have been shocked. Embracing this open-mindedness for all things seen and unseen was simply a part of my everyday life, and it informed my perceptions of all I experienced. As such, I have to take into account the culture in which disbelieving people were raised, whether it be a culture of fear or a culture that condemns what we purport to provide.

The concept of skeptics often gets conflated with that of cynics, which is a disservice to bona fide skeptics. A cynic is someone whose mind is already made up—lock, stock, and barrel—not to believe under any circumstances what their own eyes and ears are telling them. They have firmly closed the door on possibilities for taking a know-it-all position on anything mystical or unusual that can't be readily explained. Cynics tend to be very pragmatic and concrete, aligning themselves with scientifically-measurable outcomes, which is fine and well. But even when presented with truly extraordinary evidence, they will attempt to poke holes in it in order to satisfy their own disbelief. Or they may deflect from the truth by descending into a debate using "what-about-isms" to support their agenda. Cynics can be aggressively defensive of their position, and this often extends not just to metaphysical topics but other sectors as well. An example of this is the commenter of one of my YouTube videos who singled out a statement I made while channeling an audience member's loved one during a psychic gallery.

During the gallery event I was channeling a young man, and I had asked if the deceased individual and the audience member's son (who were cousins of one another) were of similar age. The YouTube comment dismissed me, stating "Cousins are usually the same age. Typical leading the witness. You can't talk to dead people!" So, out of a thirteen-and-a-half-minute video, the commenter singled out one brief question but disregarded the remainder of the exchange—a rather compelling clip if I may say so, and all of which was later validated by the deceased man's mother, who was not present but also responded to the video. Always one to give the benefit of the doubt, I suggested he just factor out the portion in question in lieu of the rest of it but that didn't satisfy him either.

The two foremost types of vehement deniers are those who accuse psychics of being scam artists and those who use the Bible to defend their position. The former group seems to have been influenced by the stereotype of the so-called fortune tellers, found along the seashore boardwalk or on the carnival fairgrounds, who read palms or tea leaves. I've always been of the opinion that you have to take into account the environment before drawing conclusions about the legitimacy of the reader. In other words, I would sooner interpret the carnival reader as a "just-for-fun" entertainment rather than someone who is truly authentic given the circus-like atmosphere. And to be fair to the accusers, there's a long and sordid history of scam artists posing as psychic readers or palmists, such as has long been characterized in movies and on TV. These types of grifters are expert at manipulating the gullible and naïve with mystic jargon, obvious speculation, and vague predictions. They attempt to scam people out of money through deliberate deception, which has stigmatized the rest of us in the same way that people make unappealing generalizations about politicians, used car salesmen, or lawyers.

In worst case scenarios—and it still occurs, believe it or not—the grifter makes false promises of a hopeful nature, and convinces their victim to return repeatedly, paying more money each time until their savings have been depleted. It's really no different from phone or e-mail scams designed to get people to fork over money; oftentimes, folks who are elderly fall prey to these ploys. The saddest part is how the psychic scammers manipulate their victims by playing upon the emotions connected to their dearly departed, telling them the deceased want them to do things that ultimately profit the scammer. In the era of social media, some grifters actually scan various outlets—including obituaries—looking for tragic situations by which they can insert themselves as a beacon of hope. And that isn't just merely unethical, it's downright criminal. In fact, skeptics have a name for grifters who do this. They're called "grief vampires." (As I said, my protocol is to suggest that my clients wait a full year before asking to connect with a recently deceased loved one. This grants a period for the soul to reacclimate to the Heavenly realm, and for my clients to work through the worst of the grieving process.)

The other type of deniers are those individuals who attempt to counter intangible evidence by weaponizing Biblical scripture. This may be more prevalent depending upon the region of the country in which you live. The deniers tend to cherry-pick certain quotes that support their contention that efforts to commune with the deceased are in defiance of God's word. What they don't realize, or what they elect to conveniently disregard, is that there are approximately 500 Biblical references to prophets and seers, most all of them positive or at least neutral. These include consultation with those who are able to forecast predictions. The New Testament is filled with extraordinary accounts of miraculous occurrences, some of which include healing or manifestations to provide for others. In fact, in John 14:12, Jesus tells us that we, as human beings, are capable of doing the works that he does and contends *greater* works shall we do. My interpretation of this is that we, too, can perform miracles if we have faith and believe it is our birthright. I am not sharing all this in order to arm you with comeback material in a debate, it is simply for your own knowledge base and awareness.

There is another drawback that frequently arises from those who would accuse us of operating disingenuously. They simply don't understand the mechanics of psychic work. They automatically assume we should know everything already; should be making predictions that evolve into fruition; or should be independently wealthy for consistently winning the lottery. They fail to realize that we often receive fragments of information and have no control over what comes through. When a psychic does not produce precise information to meet their standards of expectation, it gives the accusers fodder for pointing the finger of blame while decrying, "Fraud!" They will also continue to pivot and deflect even when confronted with evidence more clearly profound than a sequence of lucky guesses. When they can't poke holes in what you've presented because of the level of accuracy, they'll fall back on labeling it "satanic," "the work of the devil," or an insult to God.

It is probably futile to get drawn into an argument with a dyed-in-the-wool cynic. Oftentimes, the same people who weaponize Biblical scripture to their own advantage will also take an identical approach to justify their school of thought on anything or anyone that does not fit within the scope of their version of normalcy. It may grant them license to practice misogyny, racism, homophobia, antisemitism, and so on. I find this all a particularly dangerous approach, as it seems the Bible is treated by those who feel threatened as if it were law and that violators are sinners subject to punishment.

As you might imagine, such accusers are usually close-minded men but not always. Once, on my Facebook page, a young woman inserted herself by making accusatory comments. Again, trying to grant her the benefit of the doubt, I replied with a civil but firm communication stating my position but she wasn't having it. In instances such as this, I'll give the individual the opportunity to reply once more, although every time they've continued their rant. If you should encounter this kind of tirade, simply do as I did—and hit the delete button. Otherwise, it is sure to be a losing proposition from which nothing is gained; this personality type must always have the last word.

It's not our job to actively engage in a mission to convince skeptics, cynics, and other non-believers. Nor would I *want* to. We would enjoy a wonderful, utopian unity if we were all on the same page at the same time, but that's simply not realistic here on Earth. I resent it when people try to impose their beliefs on me, especially if I'm made to feel inferior or inadequate for it. It is no different the other way around. No one is obligated to accept what we do, and that's okay. I have no agenda other than to be available for those who seek me. We each need to come into our own understanding in our own way and in our own time.

People need space and time to draw their own conclusions. As you will read at the end of this chapter, that often occurs through transformative experiences that prompt an awakening Aha! moment. This is why I implore you to resist engaging in a social media war with anyone who may attack you. Instead, counteract the naysayers by setting the best example you can through ethical practice, compassionate conduct, reasonable pricing, and—perhaps most significantly—doing gratis work where and when you are able. That is, provide services at no cost to those who cannot afford it or who seem in desperate need of healing. In this manner, the deniers will be compelled to judge a tree by the quality of its fruit instead of discounting you summarily with a sweeping dismissal. Allow your gorgeous good work to speak for itself.

As a sidebar discussion to the topic of skepticism, it was very surprising to me when I was first starting out that not everyone working in this field is a nice person! I was really quite taken aback by how ego-driven and competitive some people were—it was a rude awakening, to say the least. It seemed to so completely contradict what should be our collective motivation for being in this field to begin with: to be of service to others through the employ of our spiritual gifts and talents. Unfortunately, just as in any line of business, people who are unsupportive in this regard may attempt to downplay or badmouth your contributions to their own advantage. They do this to bolster themselves while granting others reason to be skeptical of you. Rest assured, this approach will grant them no longevity except among their base followers.

Should this happen to you, you can either elect to ignore it or you can illuminate the truth by dealing directly with the source. Perhaps there were extenuating circumstances that require clarity for the benefit of both parties, and the best-case scenario will resolve a misunderstanding or miscommunication. Personally, I have never understood how competitive and territorial some other psychic practitioners can be for this simple fact: we are all unique individuals. And the great thing about being human is that your psychic gifts will manifest differently in you than they do in me. Thus, there is no justification for behavior that slights or undermines professional colleagues. In fact, I have referred clients to others whom I know have expertise in areas I do not. Isn't that the way it should be?

It doesn't happen often, thank goodness, but on occasion I have had difficulty reading someone. Sometimes it is simply the result of incompatible energy, such as when I've tried to read someone who seems jaded, distracted or does not honor the process seriously. This is an aspect of the work that skeptics don't understand. That is, your abilities are not necessarily going to manifest to the same degree or consistency with every client in the way that naysayers think it should. The handful of times this has occurred, there have been specific reasons for it, which I will list here for your information as well.

There have been readings (or rather attempted readings) in which the client projected an attitude of such great skepticism that it created a real blockage. It was like pulling teeth to get these folks to cooperate with me! My sessions are a collaborative process by which I develop a camaraderie and rhythm with each individual. But in these instances, the attitude was one of personal challenge as if to say, "You're the psychic, you tell me." The irony is that once these folks acquiesced, I learned that I had, indeed, been accurate all along. I just hadn't been as precisely spot-on accurate as these individuals wanted. As such, they had been telling me I was "off" or incorrect, which served no one.

Sometimes they deny the information, which is accurate, because they are waiting to hear enough to be convinced—all of which also defeats the process. Again, this has almost always been with men in my experience but, regrettably, it seems to give them ammunition to assert, "See, I told you so…it's all a load of bunk." One such instance occurred during a psychic gallery event. The gentleman, with whom I had been interacting, sat with his arms crossed defiantly and replied to my questions with ambiguous one-word responses. Weary, I said with a forced grin, "C'mon sir, you gotta throw me a bone here!" which broke the tension, garnered some chuckles, and helped him relax enough to verify *all* that I had been telling him had been accurate.

In other instances, I have had difficulty for clients having significant mental health issues, or being heavily medicated to the point of sedation. This is particularly disconcerting because I am oftentimes only able to be as good as someone's ability to recall. Thus, if someone's thought processes are slowed and their memories are murky, it makes developing that rhythmic rapport almost impossible. This can lead to self-doubt of your abilities and skepticism on the part of your client. In one personal example, a client's depression (and prescription medication) clearly delayed her response when I conveyed that her deceased mother was singing about bluebirds flying over the rainbow, and was sending her the Bluebird of Happiness. In reply, she said only, "Okay," leading me to think it had no relevance. But as we were concluding her session, she said she had recently been asking her mother to send her a bluebird! I almost blurted out, "Why on earth didn't you say that when I told you earlier?" So, her request of Spirit was answered but she was a bit slow on the uptake.

On another occasion in which I repeatedly struck out, my client revealed that she thought I looked tired and instead of focusing on working with me, she had been giving me a reiki treatment the entire time and unbeknownst to me! This is not only something I hadn't asked for, it's something I didn't want and it caused the session to become sabotaged. These kinds of situations are frustrating not only because we all want to do our best, we also don't want to fuel anyone's fodder for skeptical word of mouth. If you come up against such circumstances, the ethical thing to do is to stop the session, apologize, and offer a full or partial refund. Like myself, I hope it will not happen very often to you either.

The reverse of this situation is when a client is not only skeptical but downright negative. Sometimes, people come in with an attitude of entitlement as if, because they are paying you for a service, they have the right to expect it to be everything they want it to be on their terms. While it is acceptable to hold out hope, coming to an authentic psychic requires that you be willing to release such control in favor of allowing it to be whatever it's going to be. The folks who come to me with this open attitude usually receive the best sessions. But there are others who expect that they should get an on-demand service by connecting to the deceased loved of their choosing. It doesn't work that way; you'll get what you'll get—not because you want it, but because you *need* it.

I've had a few instances in which I've facilitated an amazing interaction between a client and a deceased father, for example, who stepped forward to apologize for being an abusive alcoholic and provide an explanation for his misconduct by tracing his own abusive family history. Instead of what should have been a teachable moment and a healing opportunity, I've had clients say, "Okay, well, I was really hoping to hear from my mother..." In such cases, they are blind to the inherent lessons to be learned about forgiveness, releasing of toxic resentments, and breaking old patterns in heredity. One client actually said, "I didn't expect to hear from my father and I really resent him taking up my time." Sometimes, you'll get a client who psychic-hops, meaning they see a lot of different psychics searching for what they want to hear, or sifting through the information for what they want while disregarding the rest. This is unhealthy, and can lead to them interjecting your session with, "But another psychic told me such-and-such..."

This is a trap, every bit as much as those skeptics who play "stump the psychic" by demanding to hear the "secret word" that proves you are an authentic channel. What this usually means is that they believe the reading is on their terms, not that of Spirit, and as such, their deceased loved one should be able to give you the word or object or song that will definitively prove your authenticity. Trouble is, it doesn't work that way. Remember, you are an entirely unique individual and, as such, you are not in a position to comment on what another practitioner has told someone. Similarly, you are not obligated to yield to the greedy commands of a client who is self-entitled. If this happens, you can pause the session and give the person the right of first refusal to terminate the session. What I told the woman who complained about hearing from her father was, "Would you like to end your reading? Because I'm about to." These mindsets are a surefire way to sabotage the process while also doing you both a real disservice.

In other instances, skepticism may be generated by clients who follow up with you directly (or you hear about it through the grapevine) to complain that what you predicted for them did not come to pass. If this were to happen to me, I would recommend that he or she go back and review their notes or the recording they made at the time of the original session. Because I choose my words carefully, I am certain that I would be on record as stating,

"This is one possible outcome and, if you are willing to put time and effort into manifesting it, I believe there's a strong likelihood of it happening." Remember, things rarely fall into our laps without exerting effort into making them occur. The person who feels overly deserving and prefers to be passive won't like hearing that, but it's the truth.

What you can do to largely offset encountering people like this is to be certain to provide each client, in advance, with a written summary of who you are, how you conduct your sessions, and what he or she may expect of your time together. This is taking a proactive measure to minimize any problems; inform your client to feel prepared; and poise you both for a successful time together. As I outlined in Chapter Two, my readings are an hour of which during the first half hour I explain how I do my job before saying a blessing and launching into a purely intuitive thirty-minute psychic session that almost always involves channeling one or more deceased loved ones. Halfway through, I turn the session over to my client by offering the opportunity for them to ask me questions about any aspect of their life about which they are wondering. I also ask to see hard copy photographs of loved ones living or deceased, which gives me a little something visual to "work with," and I provide a body scan, at each client's discretion, by which I give them feedback on any health-related issues in the spirit of prevention.

That's how I operate, and it's all spelled out well in advance for each client. Bear in mind that, as a practicing psychic, you're only as good as the last reading, event, or class you did due to word of mouth. In order to thrive, you can't afford to cut corners and phone it in; you've got to be as authentic as possible every time. You know how to do what *you* know how to do. You don't have to defend yourself if you believe in your heart that you possess expertise in your craft. I would never discourage anyone from continuing to grow and learn and evolve, but you do not require any degrees or certificates or any specialized training to be a psychic practitioner. It may grant you credibility or boost your confidence, but it is not necessary. Just do you, and all will be well.

I said I would conclude this chapter about skeptics by telling of a transformative turn-around that has provided me with a new friend and a series of amazing adventures. Best of all, it began with a chance encounter. In late June 2019, a colleague and I were at a television station in Harrisburg, Pennsylvania to promote a wellness center's upcoming open house. In the station's green room were a number of other people who were all waiting to be called for their respective segments of the live, on-air program. I happened to sit next to a local author who had written a book about a farm in Gettysburg which served as a makeshift hospital during the battle at Gettysburg during the Civil War. He was there with his wife and we got to chatting about ourselves and our work. This gentleman was polite, personable, and seemed intrigued when I told him of my psychic abilities.

Knowing that Gettysburg regularly attracts paranormal investigators and all manner of ghost-hunting expeditions, I offered to accompany the author on his next outing to Gettysburg to see if I could pick up on anything of interest, particularly at the farm. Given his solid knowledge base, he would be in the best position to verify anything I might tell him, as my own working knowledge of the Civil War was about limited to *Gone with the Wind*. I was pleasantly surprised when the author contacted me the afternoon of our TV station meeting. He informed me that he was, himself, skeptical but had previously experienced some unusual activity while in Gettysburg. We made a date for the following August to meet up at the farm, and I stressed the importance that he not influence me with any information in advance.

On the appointed day, he graciously followed my lead as I walked through the farm, barn and the surrounding property. It was really the first time I had ever "read" an environment in this way; my specialty is people. But I soon found myself immersed in not just the history of the site but also the *emotion* associated with it. Several times he and I both were on the verge of tears for what I was relaying. There are two floors to the barn, which served as a hospital, and I identified an upstairs area that had been designated as a space in which the deceased were laid out. There were a number of unpleasant visuals I received, including blood soaking through the second-story floorboards and leaking to the rooms below, which the author was able to confirm. I "knew" there was a terrible thunderstorm at this time; that brandy was used as an antiseptic and as "medicine" to dull the pain of soldiers' injuries; and I correctly identified a woman known as Mary who showed herself to me as a Florence Nightingale-type of nurse persona. In another instance, I picked up on a man who wasn't a doctor but served in that capacity and took a liking to being called "Doc." The author validated most all of the impressions I had received, and many that he couldn't verify on the spot, he confirmed afterwards. Most importantly, I sensed abundantly how sacred a space it was and that the average tourist didn't comprehend that aspect of the farm.

The author had audio recorded our tour and, upon debriefing together, we both regretted not bringing a videographer with us, so compelling was the testimony. It was a powerful afternoon, and we were both encouraged by it enough to set another date to visit different Gettysburg sites open to the public, but with a videographer in tow. We have since created a series of videos, now posted to YouTube, documenting our treks to such notable Gettysburg sites such as Devil's Den and the notorious Sachs Covered Bridge. The latter is reputedly one of the top ten most haunted places in the United States—a detail he opted not to reveal until after our survey of the foreboding bridge. So dense was the underlying gloom of the structure, I was unable to finish walking the length of its interior for feeling weak-kneed and nauseated. The bridge video playback showed significant audio anomalies that shouldn't have occurred, which heightened the mystery of this unusual location.

I'm sure that my treks to historical locales will continue as schedules allow. The author has been gracious in participating in the production of the videos as a personal and professional concession to me, which I both respect and appreciate. At every turn, he has expressed his great support and admiration for my work which I, oftentimes, don't feel is anything terribly spectacular seeing as how it's part and parcel of my everyday life. He has readily adapted to my style of making random interruptions as I receive information, and has honored my requests to tell me nothing about where we are going in advance so that the purity of my impressions is not tainted. (In what may have been a moment of counteractive sabotage, when we arrived at Sachs Covered Bridge an older couple pulled up in a car asking where the psychic was and started talking about certain details of the bridge to our alarm!) Throughout my many interactions, the author has reminded me that he is skeptical, which I appreciate. But, he tells me, he is willing to concede one exception where I am concerned. And for that, I am truly grateful.

Chapter 5

Self Regulation

In the first chapter of this book, I related my protocol for opening up and "turning on," so to speak. It is equally—if not more—important to be conscious of shutting down and returning to normalcy (whatever your version of normalcy may be). No one—I repeat—no one should be open and turned on all day, every day. I know it looks that way on psychic reality TV shows, but the truth is if you do not self-regulate, you risk eroding your mental-emotional, physical, and spiritual well-being—the very aspects of your personhood that I've recommended you keep at optimal attunement in order to be at your best as a practicing psychic.

I guarantee you, even the psychics on television turn on *and* turn off, though the shutting down portion of their self-regulation may never be shown or discussed. For example, a hypothetical scenario from such a program might be that the psychic goes to a hair salon for a color touch-up and while there, starts reading the colorist dyeing her hair. First of all, we've already discussed how doing this to strangers randomly is not advisable and bad form. Second, the psychic would have needed to deliberately turn on prior to entering the salon to be ready to work.

In other words, preparations were made in advance for something that appears to be unfolding very spontaneously. (Those preparations also including scouting out the location and obtaining proper releases to authorize the video crew's presence.) This is not to be misconstrued with whether or not the reading is legitimate; this is merely part of what goes on behind the scenes. Third, once the "shoot" is over, the psychic must shut down and turn off.

Why bother turning off? Suppose you didn't self-regulate in this manner—and perhaps you still don't, or didn't but learned the hard way that you must. Can you imagine trying to grocery shop, and every aisle you walk down you begin picking up on other shoppers' emotions, grievances, or even their deceased loved ones? The cumulative effect of being attuned to people in the supermarket, the gym, the post office, the bank, and everywhere else in your community—not to mention phone, e-mail, and social media interactions—could conceivably leave you fatigued and drained of your reserves of good energy.

When you deliberately and consciously turn off, after having turned on for work, you are protecting yourself and your assets. By guarding against undesired interruptions, you lessen the likelihood of anything (or anyone) causing distractions or disruptions to the quality of your life. Then you are at liberty to focus on your children, your pets, your significant other, your family and neighbors, and so on. In other words, you revert back to an average, everyday way of being. I'm not telling you not to register feelings or to behave indifferently toward others, I'm just suggesting you remain conscious and aware of how you apportion the precious reserve you've got.

Exactly how you decide to turn off is entirely up to you, but I will share my methods for doing so here. You may wish to try these or other ways best suited to yourself and your own personal style. Immediately after I am finished working, I tap the center of my forehead, or third eye, three times to signify that I am done.

Then I visualize pulling down a window shade on a business storefront, and the shade reads, "Off Duty and Closed for Business." I do this regardless of whether I have completed a series of private readings, a gallery event, or if I have been conducting a workshop. When I get home, I usually find that I am hungry, and I'll eat a snack or small meal of fruit, nuts, or vegetables. If I have time, and it's not too late, I'll go for a brisk walk too. These are tangible ways of making the turning off process both mindful and distinct.

There's one more thing I've learned through experience that I must also do, and that is: take a shower. I don't know if it's the physical act of showering or if it's symbolic or a combination of the two, but there's just something about washing clean, feeling refreshed, and sending whatever I've accumulated rinsing down the drain. I'm not sure what exactly is rinsing down the drain, but I visualize any toxins or attachments I may have inadvertently acquired sluicing off of me and being discarded. I firmly believe the water does its part to aid and restore me at this time, for I am relaxed and relieved afterwards. Then I can be free to vegetate by watching television or surfing the internet. Previously, I found that when I skipped showering, I had difficulty shutting down to sleep at night. I would toss and turn, or had unusual (but not disturbing) dreams. Once I enact this process, I am able to regroup and rebuild my personal energy reserve for the next day's work.

You may also discover that there are methods necessary to destress to add to your daily routine in order to stay grounded. Consider how to integrate aspects of mindful self-care into the everyday flow of your typical schedule. It is important to have diversions separate and apart from the work that comes of being a practicing psychic. When we are working, we're operating with, and accessing, a realm of high-vibration frequency that most others ignore or disregard. Having a foot in both worlds can be a bit of a juggling act depending upon the other obligations and priorities of the real world. Where others may cope with stress by relapsing into bad habits, think on how you might channel your decompression opportunities into something for which you hold great interest or passion.

Only you can determine what will suit you best, be it some form of exercise, arts and crafts, playing or singing music, binge-watching episodes of your favorite show, gardening, or any number of healthy options to tend to yourself and balance your needs. Remember, it is self-preservation—not selfish—to regularly incorporate self-care into your lifestyle. In this way, you are best poised to have the strength and energy to serve others. Your job is to be an impartial third party, taking an objective perspective as the intercessor, or go-between, as you relay information. When I first started out, it never occurred to me to that clients would take it so seriously as to become emotional. I quickly learned to have a box of tissues nearby! But there are times when what's being communicated in a session is so powerful that I cannot help but to be affected as well. Self-care should grant you the ability to stay balanced, especially for those who are empaths.

Empaths are individuals who are so sensitive, so compassionate, that they assume the emotional pain, suffering, and heartache of others as their own; this can also extend to include physical pain and discomfort. I have known of family members, separated by geographic distance, who simultaneously experienced stomach cramps, for instance. But only one of them actually had a diagnosis and the other was merely mirroring the symptoms, so closely aligned were they with one another. This happens to partners and spouses, close friends, and siblings—particularly twins. If you are an empath, don't allow anyone to bully you into toughening up, snapping out of it, or getting over it. The world needs sensitive people like you in it! But if you are an empath *and* a practicing psychic, you will need to take special precautions to exercise homeostasis over your mental-emotional, physical, and spiritual well-being by some or all of the methods discussed here.

As you grow your reputation beyond your town, your county, or perhaps even beyond the borders of your state, you will find yourself increasingly contacted by people who are imposing their personal agenda upon you, appealing to you in desperation to address their wants and needs. You may, initially, find this quite flattering; and, indeed it is, for it indicates the strength of your good standing and integrity. Where your work is concerned, your first allegiance is to yourself and your own well-being. This may sound self-serving to some. In my experience, I have found enacting this separation more challenging for women than men. Perhaps this is because, as mothers, women feel a special obligation as nurturers and caregivers to be present and sacrifice by doing for others. The reality is, you can't be all things to all people.

Strangers may reach out to you without notice asking you to read them at no cost. Others may want you to advise them on their love life; to pray for someone unknown to you; or tell them the location of their missing cat. People may also request that you donate your time for fundraising purposes to benefit an organization or charity that wants to raffle a reading, for example. Acquaintances may even ask if you'll do them a favor by reading the friend of a friend, or give them insight into their own investments, jobs, relationships, and so on. Some days it may seem as though everyone has coordinated to bombard you with requests and it may feel both frustrating and overwhelming. Again, this is a reflection of the high regard in which you are held. You can handle these types of requests a couple of different ways.

I have taken the approach that I am not obliged to reply to each person who contacts me with an unsolicited request. You'll recall the reference to "psychic-hoppers" I made previously; people do this online as well as in person. Personally, I don't care for it when people send me a very brief message asking me to do something for them (misspelling too) as in, "If U R physic, when will he get back w me?" It can get annoying when they follow up a few moments later with "????" as if I am supposed to accommodate their schedule when, in fact, they are imposing upon mine. Like myself, you are not a free online service. As such, you may reply by informing any requester of your services and fees, and let them know you'd be happy to schedule a private session if your terms are agreeable. Or, as I already stated, you may simply opt not to reply at all. In taking this approach, the worst thing anyone can ever say about you is that you didn't respond.

Only do gratis what you feel called to do. For example, I have the ability to relieve people of physical pain and discomfort by pulling it out of them with my hands. It's a process that takes about ten minutes. If I am giving a client a private reading and, as a result of scanning his or her body for any issues, I see that there is significant pain, I will always offer to remove it. This is also always at no additional cost and, if time does not permit, I arrange another time for the client to come to me for this service. As someone who has very rarely experienced physical pain and discomfort, I feel a certain responsibility to honor my good fortune by serving others in this manner. If the pain is chronic, meaning it's persisted for months or years, what I offer can act as a temporary anesthetic, numbing the pain anywhere from three days to three weeks or more before it slowly returns. If the pain is recent, it can be removed permanently.

Occasionally, I am contacted by people who need help in gathering information on a missing person or an unsolved homicide. If it is not a direct family member or a member of law enforcement asking, I request that the individual arrange for the proper people to make a direct request of me. For the same reason that it is bad form to approach strangers on the street to accost them with psychic information, it is equally bad form to initiate contact with the desperate or grieving family of someone missing or murdered. There is no need to actively pursue this subset of our field. If you are intended to specialize in this type of service, you will be called to it and circumstances will be such that opportunities will present themselves. If the proper people do reach out to you, you will need to determine if you are open to the challenge and willing to take on the responsibility. People of missing loved ones are not just desperate, they're raw and very impressionable. This is when language matters most and it is our place to always offer hope, not make personal judgments as to whether an individual is still living or deceased.

As part of how you regulate yourself and your time, you may wish to consider mentoring others as you grow in confidence and experience. It may happen for you, as it does to me, that you feel pulled to take someone under your wing, so to speak, as the result of a psychic reading with an individual who is on the verge of breaking through themselves. You may recognize someone as possessing tremendous potential but, oftentimes, he or she is uncertain or lacking in self-esteem, as perhaps you and I once did. As I related earlier, this is the rationale for offering the workshops that I do, but you may want to be selective in when, where, and with whom you devote your time. The greatest part of mentoring someone to hone their psychic skills is the launch, by which you can feel the almost parental pride in helping him or her to grow wings and soar. You'll have a colleague for life and you can feel certain that those whom you have mentored will pay it forward at some future point. And that's a win-win situation.

Chapter 6

A Word About Ghosts

As a practicing psychic—and especially if you are a psychic medium—it is imperative to understand your potential to encounter discarnate souls or ghosts, as they are most commonly called. What exactly is a ghost? For the purposes of making the distinction in this discussion, I'm going to delineate the term ghost from the term spirit, although they are oftentimes seen as interchangeable. I equate the word spirit to be synonymous with soul. That is, spirit is the essence of the soul that animates the human body but divorces itself from the physical form at the moment we each take our last breath. Once released from its physical form, the spirit may then make its way to the Heavenly realm to complete its transition. This process occurs in one way or another for all living things.

A ghost is identical in all respects to the preceding description except that the soul does not successfully transition to the Heavenly realm and remains here, among us, on the Earth plane. As I have learned, and as has been shown to me repeatedly, dying is not a one-size-fits-all procedure. Dying is a fact of life every bit as much as birth. Even though we all will do it, none of us dies in precisely the same manner because we are all unique individuals. Although two different people may drown, or suffocate, or pass with a fatal illness, their individual experience can only be felt by each alone. So it is that once the soul departs the body, there is a choice to be made whether to go forward or stay behind.

There are reasons for delays in the transitioning process—and all of it is contingent upon free will. As such, ghosts are actually a lot more common than people think. You might be wondering, "What would prompt the soul or spirit of a deceased person to remain here?" Again, the rationale is as unique as each person's mindset. The composition of our individual souls has in its makeup the personality of the individual. If the person was decent, kind, and an all-around good person, chances are he or she will know precisely where to go when the time comes. People who worry whether or not they've been a good person actually have nothing at all to worry about. Their concern demonstrates a consciousness for how they behave and interact with others. It's the folks who lack this degree of consciousness that may have a rude awakening.

As a general rule, it's the abundance of heavy, negative human emotions that influences the ego and precludes a spirit from progressing onward to the Heavenly realm. This includes people who conduct themselves in a counterproductive manner by feeding their own needs and manipulating others to do so. People who are selfish, greedy, insensitive "takers" know in their heart of hearts that they are not good people. They just choose not to acknowledge it and spend a lifetime in denial of the truth. These are the folks that tend to resist the reckoning that must occur when they take their last breath. What it boils down to is fear. They are afraid of being punished, being condemned, and being turned away. The heaviness of their hate, revenge, jealousy, bitterness, resentment, and ego-driven obsessions comprise the worst of human behavior. Combine this with their fear, and you've got all the makings of someone who will deny their own death, even as it's happened.

As I touched upon in Chapter Three, these people live something of a half-life, not fully human but operating and functioning in human mode while still possessing their anger. Due to their negative personas, they tend to attract to them others who are similarly "stuck." One young man, whom I aided to transition to the Heavenly realm, referenced another, belligerent man who would often come around to "bum a smoke off me." This affirms my contention that like attracts like, and this gray, murky half-existence is their version of "hell."—a lonely, desolate in-between state inhabited by others who are devoid of love, compassion, and the ability to illuminate the truth about themselves. Instead, they have lost all track of time as they attempt to mimic the routines to which they had previously been accustomed. The trouble is, most people cannot see or hear them, which only serves to heighten their agitation. The loss of bodily functions may be confusing as well though they still view themselves as they and others always have. It is for this reason that on the rare occasions they are seen, they will project an image of themselves as their consciousness recalls it to be. This makes sense when you take free will into account and my contention that when you die, you will still be you.

Does this mean that the ghost is doomed to inhabit this way of life indefinitely? Remember, this is all about free will. No one is forced to go, but the ultimate goal is for the soul in ghost state to figure it all out for themselves, and decide to depart on their own. This may account for certain environments retaining reputations as allegedly "haunted" for long periods of time, decades or a century or more in some instances. In these cases, the ghost has learned how to move (and throw) solid objects and also pass through them, such as moving through walls. They may imitate noises or voices in an effort to drive people away or to entertainingly toy with them out of boredom and malice. They may disrupt people's sleep and may even influence their thoughts negatively, especially if the person has a mental health issue or an addiction.

I have been shown that if the ghost, or earthbound soul, is stubborn and unyielding, eventually a loved one, or even an angel, with make their presence known in an effort to convince them to discard their way of life and return to the Heavenly realm. This is a pivotal moment as it requires a shedding of the vast majority of negative, divisive human emotions in favor of acquiescing to the truth. This is a process that will continue in the Heavenly realm through mentoring and rehabilitation efforts, just like here. The soul needs its damaged energy restored so that he or she may love and be loved, and relearn how to love themselves. As such, ghosts are more deserving of our empathy and pity than our fear for their rather pathetic, half-existence.

Not all ghosts have been nasty people however. As much as I would wish we could all pass peacefully in our sleep, the truth is that people die in any number of ways and some of them are very stressful and unpleasant. The acute and tense emotion associated with the death may create a psychological imprint that renders the human soul impotent for a time. I have twice been in situations in which I've investigated hauntings in which a very dominant male ghost had control over directing other, more submissive ghosts, usually women and children. In these situations, it may be that a murder-suicide event occurred and the murdered individuals gravitate toward the perpetrator out of confusion, coercion, or force of habit for being so accustomed to his controlling ways.

In other instances, people may die very suddenly and tragically, such as in a car accident. In these cases, it is easy to understand why some victims would feel disoriented. They may remain in the vicinity of the collision site, or they may attempt to go about the business of their daily habits. If you Google information on paranormal occurrences in Shanksville,

Pennsylvania in the days following the September 11, 2001 terrorist attack and airplane crash, you will learn of the testimonies from the security guards posted at the site who claimed they heard people pounding on the outside of their trailer, and actually identified victims who were running from the location of the plane's impact. I recently channeled a teenage boy who came forward during a reading with the mother of a friend of his (both boys had the same first name and played on the same baseball team). He had been killed when the ATV vehicle which he had been driving flipped and crushed him. My client told me that, the very next day, he was spotted walking through the halls at school. This doesn't surprise me but I think that usually, under such circumstances, the initial disorientation soon fades as a new understanding enters to take its place.

I'm sharing this information about ghosts because, as someone who is a working psychic, you should know these things and be prepared should you, yourself, encounter a ghost if you haven't already. You have to remember, there's no such thing as a "friendly ghost" so don't let anyone tell you they accept the presence in their home and don't mind it. Ghosts shouldn't be here, they should be *there*. And some of them can be very defensive and violently territorial when it comes to resisting attempts to get them to go *there*. The good news is that because they have been human, and still consider themselves as such, they retain their human thoughts, feelings, and emotions. What this means is that you can reason and rationalize with them in the way that you might with a child, a co-worker, or anyone else who is being unreasonably stubborn and obstinate. But the persuasive communication has to be on your terms and within the parameters you set. This is most important as I will relate to you now.

The most significant ghost experience I have had was with Travis. He appeared during a psychic gallery event, as his cousin was in the audience. I began channeling him and interpreting his messages to the female cousin on his behalf until he cursed at me. Given the vulgar way he communicated I knew in that precise moment that I was not dealing with a spirit, I was dealing with a ghost. You'll recall earlier that I declared any soul in spirit who has successfully transitioned will never swear in a manner that is degrading or defamatory; if they do curse, it will be in a teasing, lighthearted way to reveal an aspect of their personality that is readily identifiable. In my mind, I quickly shifted gears, sent Travis to a corner of the room, and told him I would deal with him when I was ready. I took back control of the event and proceeded as if nothing had happened. But before we left, I joined hands with his cousin and said a prayer for his well-being.

As I was driving home from the event, I suddenly realized Travis was hitching a ride in the passenger seat beside me! (This was before I was in the habit of limiting myself as a channel only for the duration of the event.) "Oh no," I said, "We're not doing this. I am not your ticket to feeling like you're a part of me and my life," and I mentally kicked him out. Today, of course, I love Travis but, then, the relationship was love-hate. He needed me because I was his interpreter and his vehicle for feeling connected to the real world as we know it. What I had learned about Travis is that he was the father of a little girl, and had been struggling with addiction. He had been living in a halfway house when he was shot by a housemate in an argument over a bottle of liquor. He had made me feel the hits to the stomach he received but, curiously, he never made me feel the blow to the head which killed him. This made sense, though, for his being in denial of his own death. At the time, Travis had been deceased for about a year and a half. He was 31.

Shortly thereafter, I began a long Saturday of back-to-back appointments, and the first client that morning had been in the audience for the psychic gallery event. She sat in front of Travis' cousin and told me she knew the family tangentially. As we began her session, which she recorded, there was Travis, angry and annoyed. I asked her what she wanted to do; we could address him then and there, or we could proceed with her session as planned. She opted to proceed and address Travis if time permitted. I told Travis to leave several times and, each time, he would retreat just a little bit more, standing in the room doorway, then in the hall outside the room, then on the steps to the building. My client told me that on the playback of her recording, she heard Travis cursing and growling, and there were several gunshots fired.

Imagine my surprise when the last client of the day who walked in was the cousin with whom I had interacted that night at the psychic gallery event. But, as she told me, the session wasn't for her, it was for Travis' mother, who walked in behind her! "Oh my gosh," I said, "Travis was here this morning and I kicked him out!" I cautiously began the session with Travis' mom and there he was. She, too, had been feeling as though he hadn't passed over. In fact, she and her husband were raising his daughter and a toy in her bedroom kept going off on its own, which frightened her. Over the course of the next hour, we both pleaded and coaxed and cajoled Travis into understanding the need to release his hold on this world and transition to the next. In response, he was initially defiant and accusatory, deflecting from our position by saying things like, "I can't even take a fuckin' piss," and "I miss the taste of meat." My response was to challenge him in an effort to prompt a realization within him. "Why can't you urinate, Travis?" I asked, adding, "Why can't you have a hamburger?"

By the end of the session, we had worn him down enough such that he sounded like he was considering it all. "Travis, lift up your head," I implored. "You'll see a pinpoint of light—that's the way to Heaven. Move toward it. It will get bigger and brighter, and before you know it, you'll be there." Still, he was uncertain. "How do I know I can trust you?" he countered. "Because your mother and I love you and would never deceive you." "What about my daughter?" he asked. "She'll be okay, we promise," we added. He was still wavering when we concluded our time together. I gave him a week to make up his mind before his mother and I would regroup. In the meantime, we would all be praying for him. Though he remained rather unconvinced, Travis was much calmer and more civil.

The next afternoon, I was taking a walk through the woods. I had just said my prayers and suddenly there was Travis. He was a bright light, flashing and shimmering and doing cartwheels and backflips! He hugged me and thanked me, saying, "Tell my mom that God is love," "Tell my mom she has to help other moms going through the same thing," and, perhaps most significantly, "Tell my mom she has to forgive the other guy," meaning the perpetrator of his death. This was certainly a complete reversal in attitude from the sullen, angry young man to whom I had become accustomed. As I had just said a prayer, I felt reasonably certain this was all authentic but I decided to wait a day before reaching out to his family. When I did regroup with his mother, I learned some startling news.

About an hour before my walk, Travis' mom had been laying on the bed in her room when her cell phone went off. The incoming call was from Travis' old cell phone, which was in the same room with her, resting atop his cremains on her dresser! She answered the call and only heard static noise that got louder and angrier before cutting out. Our interpretation of this was that Travis was making one last effort at the viability of his present way of life before deciding that perhaps we knew best. He had obviously crossed over and was joyous for his newfound freedom and lightness of being. I relayed my experience and all that Travis had told me. Afterward, Travis' mother did counsel another parent through a similar situation, and worked toward forgiveness of Travis' killer. Both Travis and his family were finally able to reach closure and begin to heal.

Six months later, I was stunned to learn that Travis' mother had been killed in a car accident. For some reason, I was looking at the obituaries of the local newspaper's online edition, and saw her picture. She had been driving Travis' daughter and her friend to school when she hit a patch of black ice and was thrown from the vehicle; both children were unharmed. If such a tragedy had to happen, I am so grateful that I was available to support Travis and his family before his mother passed away. Since then, Travis has appeared once or twice during other psychic gallery events, always to lend support when I'm channeling young male personalities similar to his. As such, I commend him for acclimating to his new way of being, and I hope he was able to be present to escort his own mother to the other side when it was her time.

I've shared the anecdote about Travis to underscore several things. First, if you should experience a similar situation, it is important that you gain control and disallow any ghost from taking the upper hand in what you do and say. Keep them in their place the same as would a teacher or a scolding parent; they'll have no choice but to follow your lead. Second, ghosts are not to be feared; they are enraged, upset (sometimes understandably so), and feel cheated and shortchanged. Like anyone else with what they believe to be a legitimate complaint, they want to be heard, acknowledged, and understood. Third, as I related previously, because they still retain all human attributes, except for a solid form, you can be persuasive in reasoning with them. It was in this manner, that I slowly but steadily got Travis to go where he needed to be.

Just as a loving presence in spirit will play upon the "clairs" by inputting and infusing the receptive psychic with pleasing sensory sensations, a ghost will be similarly manipulative. Except because the ghost is egotistical and upset, the sensory sensations will be unpleasant. For example, happy visuals will be replaced by violent or pornographic visuals. You may feel headachy or nauseated. Sounds heard may be guttural groans and growls, or angry, argumentative voices. Scents will be foul-smelling aromas such as garbage or sewage, or smells associated with an addictive personality such as alcohol, tobacco, or marijuana. Ghosts may even infiltrate your dreams, disrupting your sleep with nightmares in order to gain control over you. In worst case scenarios, females have felt sexually violated by a dominant male presence.

It is important to note here that they are other negative energies that can use these same tactics but are not ghosts. They are wholly evil energies with destructive agendas that would commonly be called "demons." Demonic energies may also imitate a ghost entity in order to influence you or gain your trust, such a portraying a little girl ghost who is "lost" and needs you to help her find her mommy. While these energies might mimic a human being, they are entirely inhuman and, unlike ghosts, cannot be reasoned or rationalized with. However, their Achilles' heel is that by their very nature, they are so nefarious that any illusion they manifest will be imperfect. As such, something will always be "off," and they will always get it wrong.

This is a key piece of empowering information and will aid you to distinguish the projection of a demonic energy from that of a ghost or even a loving spiritual presence. The imperfect manifestation will have the wrong eye color, will be accompanied by a noxious odor, or will be missing fingers, a hand, and so on. In more than one instance, a psychic individual, skeptical of an "angel's" harmful instructions, challenged the presence in God's name to reveal its true self. The entity promptly "unzipped" its manifesting projection to reveal its true, demonic form. These types of energies are not only unfeeling, they are callous and cowardly, and will attack children, people who are developmentally disabled or autistic, and people who are already struggling with addiction and mental illness. They will also influence the wealthy, the famous, and the powerful because those are individuals who have many followers.

You are under absolutely no obligation to entertain ghosts or combat demonic energies if you don't personally feel called to it. Some psychics do have this as an area of specialty and expertise, and feel completely comfortable, knowledgeable, and empowered to deal with these types of situations, which are becoming increasingly commonplace. It is important to be aware of the dark side and how it operates but if you would prefer to leave it at that, then take control of your own psychic settings. As part of your turning on process, cast a veil of protection over yourself and the space in which you will be working, and disallow anything that is not for the greatest good of the highest order from entering forth. If you are knowledgeable about angels, call upon those who are known defenders of human beings. If you wish to underscore these protective measures with crystals, sage, or other devices in an insulating ritual of your own design, this will reinforce the sacredness of the space. If you opt not to entertain any interaction or discussion dealing with ghosts or demons, you should have at your fingertips the necessary contact information so that you may make a referral. As I said, these situations have become extremely common and people are in need of support for feeling attacked and manipulated.

Chapter 7

Business as Usual (Not!)

In the introduction to my events, I tell people that, as a psychic medium, I don't have a normal life and I don't have a regular job. And neither do you, I'm betting! In order to market your services as a psychic, you've got to know your own abilities quite thoroughly so that you understand what you can offer, and potential clients know what to expect of you. As I discussed previously, your demographic is likely to be mainly females and a few open-minded males. You'll also need to consider the avenues through which to offer your services, and how to price what you're offering so that you are both affordable and accessible, especially if you are new to the field and haven't yet established a reputation for quality work.

In order to generate awareness for your services, you'll want to have a web site to which you may refer clients. There are ways to create your own web site at little or no cost, or, if you can afford it, you may wish to have a site professionally designed. Your smiling face should be the first thing people should see on your web site— you *are* your brand. It will immediately identify you and set prospective clients at ease by demystifying yourself as an ordinary person with an extraordinary ability. Your web site should also provide a biography with your background; a description of your services and fee schedule; and how people may contact you for further information and to set up an appointment. Make sure that the phone number you give out is not a home number used by your family but your own cell phone number. It is also helpful to have a presence on social media and your web site should directly link to your account pages. You may also wish to create a blog on your web site by which you may communicate thoughts and experiences you'd like to share; keep it informal but professional. It's otherwise probably best not to share details about your personal life including names and ages of your children so that you maintain a professional distance. Your web site may also display your schedule of upcoming events and locations of such.

You may initially feel reticent to charge money for your psychic services but you *must*. If you make yourself available at no cost, you are setting yourself up to be used, abused, and manipulated in a co-dependent relationship. You'll also upset a lot of other psychics, card readers, and other metaphysical practitioners in your area for taking away their business or, at the least, not creating a competitive market of available services. Everyone needs to earn a living, and there's no good reason why you shouldn't charge reasonable rates the same as anyone else is fairly compensated, is on salary, and receives a paycheck. So even though you're a gifted psychic, you're under no obligation to give it away except in those instances you are called to do gratis work, as was discussed before. Other people in other professions are gifted at what they do too, and they make an income doing it. You are no different.

Decide what you can make available to your clients based on who you are and what you do. Are you going to offer private, in-person and one-on-one sessions? If so, will you allow more than one person to be present at a time? I often have people ask if their sister, friend, or husband can "sit in" on their private session. My position on this is a firm "no" for a couple of reasons. First, if there's someone else in the room, their energy could possibly interfere with my ability to focus exclusively on the paying client, especially if the other person is too talkative, interrupts, or even commandeers the session. That could be disastrous to the client, your reputation, and the outcome of the session altogether. The second reason I decline is that I don't wish to set a precedent that others can squeeze in on a "two-for-one" type of deal in which both parties have the opportunity to fully participate for the price ordinarily charged a single person. Like anything else, once I make an exception, word will travel quickly and others will want it—and may want to add people to the mix too. If you decide to do this, you should increase your fee accordingly to account for the extra person.

You may determine how long your sessions will last, if you wish, depending upon the needs of your clients. You can see clients for 15, 30, or 60-minute increments if you so choose; although 15-minute increments are probably not practical unless you're offering this timeframe long distance by phone or via an online video or audio platform. A 60-minute session is usually the norm unless someone has a very specific topic to discuss in a 30-minute timeframe. At one time, I had offered 30-minute "brush up" sessions for folks in between their annual, one-hour appointments. Personally, I've never conducted a session longer than 60 minutes because I haven't felt it necessary. I believe all that needs to be addressed with a client can be done in that period of time, but there may be extenuating circumstances for which you may want to extend a session to 90 minutes by mutual agreement with a client and adjusting your fee accordingly to reflect such.

If you are practicing in your own home, there's no overhead except your own utilities for home office space., so you may adjust your fees to reflect this. However, I strongly suggest you not see clients in your own home for a few reasons. The first is most important, and that is to separate your private life from your professional life. Unless you have the luxury of a private office room that is business-like in appearance, there's too much potential for aspects of your personal life to seep over as distractions and interruptions. This may range from the intrusions of pets and children to responding to knocks at your front door from deliveries, neighbors, and solicitors of various kinds.

It is also desirable to preserve a measure of insulation between your personal and professional lives. This grants you some anonymity in order to protect your home life and your family. Remember, you have the potential to attract people who are very desperate and needy. Also, the average client is going to be quite nervous for not knowing what to expect. Others may have mental and physical health issues of varying degrees. Do you really want to bring such an assortment of energies into your home? Do you really want everyone to know where you live? Believe it or not, there's been a few occasions for which I've had individuals stalking me, reinforcing my relief that my home phone number and address are private. No one should be that accessible such that people might feel at liberty to show up on your doorstep during off hours and when they are not scheduled to be there. If you want to play it safe and not have clients in your home for in-person sessions, you can still provide readings from your home.

I remember a school text book, circa 1972, that had an illustration of a communication device from the future that was like a video-telephone combination by which both parties could see and speak with one another simultaneously. That prediction came to pass and in the internet age, we are blessed with technology and online platforms by which we can connect with others from all over the world and in real time. This opens up a realm of possibilities where providing your psychic services is concerned. I have, myself, done psychic readings with clients from all over the world in this manner; it's the next best thing to being there live and in person! Plus, it grants you great flexibility in scheduling, including evenings and weekends.

Best of all, you can simply conduct your sessions in the same way that you ordinarily would. The distance is of no consequence, as you are focusing on energies not bound by the laws of physics. All you need is a mobile device such as a tablet, laptop, or cell phone, and an internet connection, and you're ready to roll. As an alternative (or in addition) to online readings, you may also offer phone sessions as well. Personally, I find reading by phone challenging for not having a visual with which to "work," meaning an image of the person with whom I am speaking. But, requesting a clear photo in advance usually solves that problem.

If you don't work out of your own home to conduct private, in-person readings, the other option is to rent space. If you rent space in an office building or industrial park-type setting, you've got to have about a year's worth of rent saved up prior to the launch of your business in order to sustain until you establish yourself and can generate a steady and somewhat predictable income. If you go this route, you've got to be all-in and totally committed to who you are and what you do as it will consume most of your time, same for anyone who is self-employed. Once you establish yourself, it's got to be a viable enough prospect that renting office space makes good sense for making an income that regularly exceeds by 50% or more the cost of your rent.

An alternative to renting office space is to approach an already established yoga studio or holistic wellness center to inquire about renting space. Renting space to various wellness practitioners is a chief source of income for such businesses, and you may be surprised at how receptive the business owner may be to your proposal. The business owners with the most integrity will expect you to read them first to ensure that what you offer is indeed authentic enough to be a "good fit" with their place of business. This is standard practice, and you might even initiate offering the "screening" session yourself, which will reflect well on your own integrity. I thought I bombed my first test screening with a wellness business owner, but she saw something there— enough to offer me an opportunity that transformed my life. Be aware, too, that the same business may also rent space to other types of readers. If you'll recall my prior discussion for being undistracted by so-called competition, you'll pay this no mind in favor of focusing on what it is you know how to do.

The wellness business owner may negotiate with you a set fee by which you rent space on a monthly basis, or you might reach an agreement by which you give a percentage of your earnings to this person. Anywhere from 20-30% is often the norm. This will also guide you in setting your fee schedule, knowing that a portion of each service you offer goes toward paying the rent. Believe it or not, I've never had a written contract with any wellness center owner from whom I have rented space; it's all been verbal agreements with no problems whatsoever. This may not be the standard, however, and you may be expected to sign a contract or memorandum of understanding that states the commitment of both parties and the duration of time to be honored, usually in annual increments. The business owner may also request that you not associate with a similar business within a particular radius, which can range from 10 to 25 miles. This is to protect the exclusivity of what you are offering unique to this particular establishment, like a no-compete clause in other business contracts.

The advantages of being affiliated with a wellness center are many. You'll be able to work during regular business hours without revealing your own street address, as you would if seeing clients in your home. You'll belong to a space frequented by any number of "woke" folks in local and surrounding communities, so your visibility is greatly enhanced. These patrons may be coming for other services, such as massage or reiki, but they will be exposed to what you offer if your services are visibly posted. The center will likely add you to its web site as one of its practitioners, which will greatly aid your credibility in getting established, as people may recognize you for being affiliated with a particular place of business that has a good reputation. Similarly, you can link to the center, and they to you, on your social media accounts. This will be a good way to cross-promote one another, as you will be introduced to the center's online followers and they to yours based on your mutual promotions and posts. You will find your name recognition increasing as people tend to associate you with a particular holistic wellness center.

The center may have periodic open house or fund-raising events which will also give you the opportunity to meet-and-greet people unknown to you while offering them a sample of what you do (usually 15 minutes in duration). There's great potential to book new clients for full-length appointments as a result. Also, larger, better-established wellness centers often host an annual or biannual faire or expo event. This is an enormous undertaking that requires a lot of preparation and planning. The event is usually held off site in a rented community center or fire hall or other large venue with substantial space. Tables or booths are rented to practitioners of various modalities and wares to offer. Expos are typically held on a Saturday or over the entire weekend. Local events such as these can attract anywhere from 1,000 to 3,000 or more during its course. Again, your participation will further boost your visibility to any number of people previously unknown to you.

How much you charge for your services is something you will need to determine based on several factors. If you are working from your own home, you can probably afford to charge a little less for not paying rent. If you are paying rent, you'll need to pad your fee schedule to reflect such. Either way, you'll also need to take into account the need to pay self-employment tax out of your earnings, but more on taxes shortly. If you are just starting out, a fee for a one-hour session in the upper two digits is reasonable. If you have good word of mouth and you have repeat business, that tells you that you are affordable and accessible to your community. If you live in a more affluent community or you are marketing yourself to such, you can probably afford to charge more. I have seen psychics who have had significant media exposure charging hundreds of dollars—sometimes over a thousand dollars—for a single session, which I consider outrageous for pricing themselves out of reach of the average person.

As you cultivate your clientele and hone your gifts, you can gradually and periodically raise your fees to something in the lower three-digit range. Try to adjust your fees to coincide with the start of a new year and give your clients plenty of notice for the upcoming change. This is fair and reasonable, and in keeping with a salary adjustment that reflects inflation. After all, you are your own boss. If you are truly gifted, you will want to bear in mind the desire to keep yourself as affordable to as many people as possible so that you aren't accused of the price-gouging stereotype and to work as steadily as possible. To date, since 2004, I have raised my rates twice.

To protect yourself legally, I recommend that you include on your web site and social media accounts a written disclaimer that holds you harmless for choices a client may make of his or her own free will based upon the intuitive information you are providing. (This is also why your language matters in terms of stating "may" versus "will," for example.) Here's the disclaimer that I've used for years now. You may wish to use it, or your own version of it, on anything you post which advertises your services.

DISCLAIMER: Your psychic reading is subject to your own personal interpretation. The information provided does not constitute legal, psychological, medical, business, or financial advice. Each client receiving a psychic reading is responsible for his or her own choices and actions. Psychic readings are for entertainment purposes only.

This language is fairly standard and although you may be uncomfortable with the last line, it is necessary in order to make the distinction that you do not function in the capacity of a psychiatrist, psychologist, therapist, attorney, physician, or financial adviser.

Beyond psychic readings, you will also work more steadily if you diversify the range of what you are able to offer. You can do double duty, and increase your income, if you are trained or equipped to provide other services. I have found that most people willing to pay for a psychic are hoping to connect with a deceased loved one who has passed on. If you are a psychic medium, you will probably find this to be true of your clientele. Are you also reiki certified? Are you massage therapist? If so, that expands your ability to earn an income. It's just important that you create a mental separation in your work even though it's entirely possible to be receiving intuitive impressions while providing massage or reiki. I'll address this in detail in the last chapter of this book.

Personally, I am passionate for conducting psychic gallery events as I discussed previously in detail. It is a powerful experience to gather together a group of people for a shared experience that encompasses laughter, tears, and a unique perspective perhaps previously unconsidered. Decide how you wish to structure such an event if you feel capable of it. Know that in smaller groups, there is greater pressure, if not an expectation, that each person will receive a direct message channeled from a loved one. In larger groups, this is not always possible and you will wish to state this in your materials advertising the event. However, I am confident that, as a shared experience, everyone will come away with something upon which to reflect in the days following the gallery.

If you become adept at facilitating psychic gallery events, you may find yourself in the position of fielding requests for special events in settings outside of a wellness center. I enjoy working in theatrical settings and, oftentimes, larger theaters have a smaller space called a black-box theater which is ideal for more intimate gatherings. If this appeals to you, you may be able to negotiate an event with the theater manager. Two likely scenarios are that the theater will either accept a ticket split with you based on the ticket price, which the theater collects, as may be the case in your relationship with other venues. Otherwise, the theater will offer you the space for rent, and you will need to determine if it makes financial good sense when you take into account the costs of advertising and promotion.

Either way, you will be required to enter into a contractual agreement with the theater that specifies the agreed upon date, time, and duration of the event, as well as how you wish to be billed. Also specified will be the ticket price and the agreed upon percentage split (if there is such an arrangement). The contract will also address your needs, including audio-visual and lighting. This aids the theater to plan how many staff they'll need on hand for the event, either to set up and tear down or to provide assistance during the event itself. For example, I request to be wired with a remote "lapel" microphone, the speaker of which clips to my shirt collar and the battery pack of which clips to the belt around my waist. I also request that two staff be present as "runners" for the duration of the event to man hand-held microphones so that audience members may be clearly heard by all. Many such staffers in theaters are community volunteers.

It is also commonplace for theaters to require that you provide them with a copy of an insurance policy that covers what's called "Commercial General Liability Coverage." While such insurance is standard, it is usually used for touring performance groups such as rock bands and other theatrical or musical groups. The insurance would protect the theater from liability for damage resulting from performer or crew injuries as well as structural damage from scenery and special effects, such as any pyrotechnics for example. It's possible you might negotiate with the theater manager to waive the insurance, as has occurred on occasion for me, by explaining that your "act" is simply you standing in front of an audience. Consult with the insurance agent with whom you presently have automobile or homeowner's insurance to inquire about rates and insurers who offer this kind of policy. If you decide to acquire this type of insurance, you'll want to factor the cost into the ticket price, depending on how many such venues in which you appear per year.

A theatrical venue will be a good opportunity to build your reputation, but you have to feel comfortable speaking in front of larger groups of people and be able to deal with the pressure of meeting people's high expectations, including those skeptics in attendance. If you struggled through speech class in school for having a phobia of public speaking, you'll need to overcome this in order to be at ease before an audience of significant size. It's really where the rubber meets the road, as everything you do and say plays out in front of any number of people instead of one-on-one, as in a private psychic reading. Suffice it to say, if you have stage fright, a theater setting is not the venue for you. But if you feel you have something important to offer various communities at large, and you're a bit of an extrovert (perhaps you sang in school chorus or performed in plays), then by all means you should pursue it. If you are a great success, the word of mouth is priceless.

You may also be contacted to appear at house parties, birthday parties, Halloween parties, and other, less-formal settings. These situations are ideal for not needing to share the proceeds with anyone but yourself. It is important, though, that you adhere to your standards, and structure the event as you would in a more professional setting. I have had to insist on a "no alcohol served before or during the event" policy based on personal experience. On the one occasion it occurred, it degraded my ability to authentically read people, and their ability to recall and respond was significantly dulled. Of course, you will wish to visit the location in advance to ensure your own comfort level and to see if your requests can be sufficiently honored.

It is also important that your hosts understand that you are not "an act" in the way of a mentalist. A mentalist is a performer who entertains others by making highly intuitive deductions that seem like mind reading, and who may hypnotize audience members; may appear to bend or move inanimate objects; and who may use photographic memory or expedient calculating skills to shock and awe his audience.

I would also advise, based on personal experience, that you avoid working in a restaurant setting unless you will clearly be seen and heard by all, and only if food is served after your event. I have seen it done in which the psychic will "travel" from table to table, giving each table its own mini-session. If food (and alcohol) is being served before or during your event, there is an extreme amount of extra noise and many distractions for patrons getting up and down to use the restrooms.

If you are attuned to animals, you can offer pet readings. Animal lovers very much enjoy the opportunity to gain insights for what their beloved pets are thinking and feeling. I never thought I was capable of doing this until I realized it works the same way with animals as it does with people! It's simply tuning into their energy, gaining their trust, and swapping imagery, thoughts, and feelings. After all, telepathy is their native tongue for largely existing in silence anyway. I have found that a 15-minute session is plenty of time to hear out a client's pet and give that person a chance to ask a few questions. Animals can be quite direct and humorous, and often spill the beans on the bad habits of their owners as well as expressing their concern for the well-being of the owners. If you become adept at it, there's a whole other facet of this field that can open up to you that could involve locating lost and missing animals as well.

If you have a keen interest in paranormal topics, you might try contacting a local ghost hunters' group to see if they'd be interested in collaborating with you. There's likely little to no income to be gained from this, as most paranormal investigation teams do not charge for their services. But it will be good experience if it interests you, and all reputable paranormal investigators use psychics to grant them objective insight and perspective, to validate their findings, and to facilitate an interaction with the ghost or other entity. Should you decide to explore this, please revisit the chapter in this book on ghosts. Remember, too, that in my experience, anytime I have encountered demonic energies, there has always—without exception—been abuse and addiction in the household in which paranormal activity is occurring. So, you will need to decide if you are strong and capable enough to handle this type of situation. If so, please take care to protect yourself spiritually, and to similarly empower those under siege without enabling them further.

If you have an area of special interest, you may wish to develop a presentation, workshop, or training to educate and inform the community. This is a way to enhance your reputation; reflect well on the venue in which you present; share information and wisdom you have gained; and expand the knowledge base of others. You may get a sense for areas of interest as potential presentation topics based on feedback from your clientele. This will ensure a core group of individuals who would be willing to register in advance and spread word of mouth to others. People tend to gravitate to any opportunity that is experiential and hands-on. People also love take-aways, that is, pieces of information they can take home and begin implementing effective immediately. Consider these points when crafting what you'd like to present. Set objectives (what you wish to accomplish) and outcomes (what you want folks to learn) the same as an educator creates lesson plans for her students. This will help you to stay focused on what you wish to communicate. If you are successful, you can expand your scope of offerings in keeping with what people are requesting. One regret I've had is that every time I've offered an intuition class for kids and teens, I can't seem to generate enough interest in it, although I'm still optimistic.

You'll need to decide early on how you'd like to receive payment from clients or a third party such as the proprietor of a wellness center. Using a square device to attach to your cell phone is a quick and easy way to accept credit card payments, but be sure to adjust your rates to account for the extra percentage assumed by the card company, otherwise you're deducting that cost from your fee in addition to any rent you are making. If you receive cash, you may give cash or write a check to pay your rent depending upon the arrangement you have with the proprietor. I would advise against accepting personal checks from clients; it only takes one bad check to tarnish your willingness to receive payment this way. If you are making long-distance readings using an online platform, you may receive payment by check mailed to you in advance (which must obviously clear before you provide service) or by an online financial platform that makes a direct deposit into your bank account, which is attractive for its immediacy while allowing clients to pay by credit card if they choose.

Regardless of the manner in which you receive payment, you'll need to document your income for the purposes of formally reporting your income and paying your taxes. It is best to be organized about tracking this information so you are not scrambling at the last minute come tax time. I recommend you set up an annual spreadsheet by which you enter the date, the person or organization that made the payment, and the amount earned. If you do this immediately after each time you complete a job, you'll stay up to date. If you are working a day of private sessions from home, indicate this and simply enter the total amount earned for the day. If you are self-employed, I suggest you file taxes and make estimated payments on a quarterly basis. This enables you to project your earnings for the year while paying tax in installments instead of remitting payment all at once. Remitting your income tax all at once can be an unpleasant reality-check on your budget if you haven't projected your earnings and what you'll owe, and set aside funds for such. You'll also want to budget how much, if anything, you allot for advertising your services through print or online media, or whether you'll simply rely upon good word of mouth.

You should also have a spreadsheet that reflects the round-trip mileage you've traveled for anything work-related, such as driving to a specific location to conduct an event or hold private sessions. As with tracking your income, enter the date, the location from which you began the trip to the location of your destination. Also enter your starting mileage, on your vehicle's odometer, and the ending mileage upon your return home. Business-related travel is deductible if you are self-employed. Also deductible are business-related expenses such as office supplies, advertising fees, and charges for online social media platforms used by you to promote your business and your events. Keep a file folder marked with the tax year to hold any hard copy receipts; keep an e-file to hold any electronic receipts although I always recommend printing out a hard copy of all-important paperwork. If you are uncertain as to what qualifies as deductible expenses, consult with an accountant through online or in-person services. If you are not a mathematical whiz, you'll need an accountant (or someone adept at calculating self-employment tax returns) regardless. Be certain to download the necessary forms by which to report your federal, state, and local income tax annually or quarterly, and you'll have in place all that you require to pace yourself financially. (All federal tax forms may be found at www.irs.gov.) The better organized you are, the less stressed and frazzled you'll be come tax season.

Any business for whom you have done freelance work over the course of the year, such as making a presentation, holding a workshop, or conducting a psychic gallery, should issue to you a 1099 tax form. The business is required to do so if you have earned a minimum of $600 from them. In such instances, you are not an employee of the business but what's called a sub-contractor. This means you are a third party with whom they have done business on a one-time or periodic basis. In order for the business to issue your 1099, which reflects your earnings, they should have you submit to them a W-9 form, which indicates your name, address, Social Security number, and whether you are an individual or an entity such as an LLC (Limited Liability Company). This is standard practice and will aid you when compiling your tax information.

To conclude this chapter, and bring to a close the nuts-and-bolts portion of this book, let's address the concept of being represented by an agent. If you are truly outstanding in your psychic abilities; have an accuracy rating of about 90-99%; and have a respectable following of 1,000 or more, you may be able to interest a talent agent into representing you. Finding the proper person may be a challenge, however. Most entertainment agents—and that's the type of individual you'd need—represent actors, models, comedians, keynote speakers, magicians, singers, and bands. There is no one that exclusively represents psychic mediums because it is a burgeoning and specialized field and there simply isn't a high-end demand for it, but that may change as psychics become even more popular. Still, it can only help your visibility to be pictured and listed on a talent agent's web site. The caveat is that people may mistake you for being an entertainer, along the lines of a mentalist, and not take you as seriously as you would wish.

To locate a talent agent, you may do an internet search or peruse an employment connection web site, which is just what I have done. A lot of speaker- and talent-booking agencies don't actively pound the pavement tracking down employment opportunities for their roster; they wait to be approached about booking a certain individual with background and expertise that would complement an event being planned. As in an arrangement with a theatrical venue, the agent will typically take 25-35% of the gross income, which may also factor in administrative fees. The administrative fees would include time spent making phone calls, e-mailing, and executing paperwork (including contracts) on your behalf.

You will likely need to audition for an agent with a reading, and provide him or her with a press kit and what's called a sizzle reel. The press kit would contain a condensed version of what should already be on your web site: a crisp, clear and recent photo of yourself (called a head shot); a brief bio; a list of your accomplishments including anything you've published; and about half a dozen or so blurbs, which are one- or two-sentence quotes of endorsement from people who can attest to your prowess as a psychic and are willing to list their full name and title. Having people blurb you who are prominent in their respective field (preferably the spiritual and holistic field) grants you credibility in the eyes of the layperson. A typical blurb might read as follows: "I've had Jen at my center for psychic readings and other events, and I can tell you she's the real deal! Everyone has been amazed and we plan on having her back again soon!" –Crystale Aura, owner of Crystale Aura Wellness Center. Provide the agent with your press kit electronically in PDF format so he or she may readily post it online or send it out as needed.

A sizzle reel may take a bit more effort to pull together if you are not particularly tech-savvy. The sizzle reel comprises what is in your press kit but also includes video samples of your work. This is the primary opportunity to really sell yourself and show exactly who you are and what you do in terms of command of your craft, personal style, and authenticity. In essence, your sizzle reel should demonstrate in the space of about six minutes your "greatest hits." You want to include video excerpts of your "wow!" moments from private readings as well as other events, such as a psychic gallery, pet readings, or whatever your specialty may be. To do so requires planning in advance to have someone present willing to capture you on video and to obtain written releases from people willing to be photographed as participants.

The releases would document that the individuals being photographed grant you permission to use the video material in which they appear for a specific purpose, and includes their full name signature, and date, as well as your countersignature. All parties should receive a copy of the release form, and it may even be wise to have a witness sign as an impartial third party. Once all video material has been gathered, you'll need the final, completed sizzle reel to be edited to look slick and professional. If you cannot do this, there are photographers, videographers, and companies that can do this for you depending upon how much you wish to invest in it.

If the agent is impressed, he or she may offer to add you to their roster. This may require entering into a written agreement up front, or on a work-for-hire basis, which means a contract would be arranged once there's a job offer made. Bear in mind that for agent representation to be viable, you have to be consistently outstanding as a psychic. Any work that is offered to you will likely be larger, money-making opportunities such as corporate parties and theatrical events involving several hundred or more in attendance. (No agent will bother with anything smaller that you could set up on your own.) You have to be able to hold your own and have a command of the room in order to take control, set a tone for your work (that can include humor, mind you!), and be prepared to field skeptical heckling should it arise. The work you do will be a reflection not just of yourself but also the agent representing you. If this sounds daunting to you, you're not yet ready for it. If it sounds exciting, please proceed!

Advantages of having an agent who believes in you are that they negotiate pricing and run interference on your behalf; you are aligned with a professional agency, which may grant you some prestige and legitimacy in the eyes of others; and they should conduct themselves with professional integrity in all their dealings as your representative. Having said that, I will share that, to date, I have seven agents and only one of whom has actually lined up work for me consistently. There's simply not a demand as yet for psychics to generate enough interest such that a talent agent is necessary. But I suspect that will all be changing in the near future as people become more open and interested in what we do.

Part 2

Words of Wisdom

Preface

Now that the practical logistics of being a practicing psychic have been reviewed, I'd like to offer you a touchstone, mantra, or grounding meditation in the second part of this book. In Chapter One, I discussed the process, and importance, of turning on. I also discussed my lifestyle, by which I work to be as clear and clean and authentic a channel as possible. Some of us don't have the luxury of time to devote to doing this regularly for working a full-time job, having innumerable distractions, or honoring family commitments. I will contend, however, the importance of staying grounded is essential, especially when opening up and preparing to do psychic work. I have shared the specific ritual I enact before conducting private readings or before a psychic gallery event which involves summoning my Spirit Guides and allowing people's loved ones permission to speak through me. Well-known psychic medium John Edward has stated that he recites the Rosary prior to his events. The following 12 chapters provide an opportunity for you to reflect inward, to remain humble, and to elevate your spiritual awareness for the significance of the work to which we have committed ourselves.

Curiously, this portion of the book begins with a book. In August 2016, I bought a children's book from the 1920s. As I was leafing through my purchase, I discovered a bookmark. This was not an ordinary bookmark, nor was it commercially printed. It was, instead, homemade. In fact, I believe it is also of the 1920s era. The bookmark is of purple construction paper, the kind of paper schoolchildren might use. With time, the purple has faded to mauve and has taken on a slight tan color at the edges. What makes this piece of paper remarkable is not what it is but what is on it. In writing, down the left edge, is a ruler measurement carefully scribed in indigo fountain ink. The measurement is delineated in "inches" that are not real inches but roughly half-inches. Corresponding to each "inch" is a word or a phrase, so that there are 12 altogether. At the top of the bookmark is written the title, "Love's Foot Rule."

As I examined the bookmark more closely, it seemed to have indeed been crafted by a child, probably a schoolgirl of about 10 or so, judging from the neatness of the script. It occurred to me that each of the 12 "rules" in Love's Foot Rule were aspirations for this child. Ultimately, they are tenets for all of us to abide by in daily life. By referring to such a tangible reminder in the form of a bookmark, we might remain conscious and aware for the importance of each entry, and the desire to embrace each to the best of our ability. In fact, I have reflected upon Love's Foot Rule to prepare for private sessions with clients and before the start of psychic gallery events. It aids me to reflect inward and get my head in the right space for authentic channeling.

Curiously, I became less interested in the book and more intrigued by the bookmark. Periodically, I found myself pausing to reflect on Love's Foot Rule and each of its "measurements." Again, each entry is distinguished by a single word or short phrase, but none are defined. The reason for this became apparent: the meaning for each is a purely personal interpretation, defined according to one's own mores, values, beliefs and standards. As such, in each succeeding chapter, I will reveal more intimate details of my own personal history and background.

Furthermore, I began to ponder on how I would, myself, explain each component of Love's Foot Rule. I contemplated not only the definitions but how they applied to my life, my experiences, and what it was I desired for both. This was not once and done either; contemplating Love's Foot Rule became a meditative habit. On occasion, the explanation for each entry came so fluently, so articulately, that I was compelled to jot it all down and retain it for future use. So often did this occur, I almost felt as though I was taking dictation as the words flowed and impressed themselves within my thoughts in a continuous channeling of information.

I now wish to share the result of those musings: words to consider, words to reflect upon, and words to live by if you so choose. We live in turbulent times in which grace, etiquette, and common courtesy have degenerated and become eroded. This humble little offering is intended as a contribution to the antidote for what ails us. Love's Foot Rule provides opportunities for self-reflection as we strive to become improved versions of our old selves. Your consideration of these 12 tenets will aid you to preserve professional decorum and maintain integrity where your psychic work is concerned. You are cautioned not to become overwhelmed or dismissive of the tenets as insurmountable. Instead, process each with deliberation in your own time and at your leisure. Remember, if a little girl of the 1920s set these themes as her personal goals, so can you.

Chapter 8

Long Suffering

Long-suffering: having or showing patience in spite of troubles, especially those caused by other people.
—Oxford Dictionary

When I think about the term long-suffering, I think about the seven or eight years I spent being abused in my youth. It was the most prolonged, painful period of my entire life, one that nearly drove me to take my own life. In childhood, I was the eldest of four boys. As the first child, I was indulged and fawned over. You can see me almost projecting an attitude of entitlement in photographs taken at four and five and six. As an adult, a chance encounter with someone highly intuitive offered me a truism that perfectly applied, I thought. She said that prior to this lifetime, I had known wealth and celebrity and that I am here to learn emotion. This made a lot of sense, as in this lifetime I have been humbled, am unconcerned with money, and have no desire for fame whatsoever.

As I grew and matured, I became socially awkward, physically uncoordinated, and drawn to academic interests that were not typical of my peers. This didn't really become noticeable until about the fifth grade when I was 11. It was at this age that my same-age peers started to become less inclined toward childish things and more sophisticated, more apt to judge and critique.

Because I was not athletic, I was not adept at kickball played at recess with the other boys. I mostly watched or wandered the playground. I must have stuck out like a sore thumb and I was largely shunned by my classmates. In particular, one made me his personal whipping boy, for reasons that will probably always elude me. I cannot fathom what I ever did to him. I honestly don't recall ever having a conversation with him. But he disliked me intensely and would verbally taunt me and physically harass me on a virtually daily basis. This I endured for many years.

As each August drew to a close, I would feel ill at the thought of the impending new school year; summer vacation had been my reprieve from the abuse. But, sure enough, it would start all over again in a renewal of the vicious cycle. Things seemed to escalate in junior high school when my tormentor, in essence, set an example for others to join in, and I became an easy mark. Not only was I verbally and physically abused, my speech and body language were publicly mocked and mimicked in front of cafeteria staff, school bus drivers and teachers who did nothing of significance to intervene.

In one instance, I remember returning to a classroom while classes were still in session, so the halls were empty, or so I thought. As if on cue, my primary assailant was suddenly behind me, punching me in the back as I tried to walk away. I was so passive that the thought of fighting back was not a consideration. However, in my hand I grasped a pencil and I momentarily fantasized about turning around and impulsively thrusting my pencil into his gut. I can only imagine, though, the ramifications had I done so—which may have included entering the juvenile justice system. But, unbeknownst to me, by then I was already enrolled in another system of sorts.

Shame and embarrassment prevented me from seeking support within my immediate family. I didn't want to confess that I really was that different and that I was the object of harassment. Instead, I began to reflect back what others projected upon me. I became hard and ugly, bitter and cynical. As the oldest of four boys, I became especially controlling of my brothers, perpetrating similar physical and verbal abuse. I also entered into a downward spiral of mental illness. I became severely depressed, which manifested itself not only in irritability and agitation but increasing social isolation, crippling low self-esteem, insomnia, and bed wetting. I also developed what I now know to be post-traumatic stress disorder, the symptoms of which were acute anxiety tied to the school environment; distrust of adults in authority; hypervigilance or feeling "on-guard"; and a dislike of being physically touched. The symptoms of depression stemming from this period in my life have persisted to this day.

Those who have also suffered injustices that are unreasonable or inhumane may be considered long-suffering. Often, those injustices are founded in hate and prejudice. We may further define the experience of long-suffering as being discriminated against and oppressed but unwilling to yield one's core principles. It is the process of enduring many hardships knowing that spiritual grace ultimately reconciles inequities, although we may not witness it in our lifetime. To sustain, one must be true to one's self, and hold fast to the knowledge that compensation will come once the truth is illuminated. This is what transpired for me, personally, as you will read further on.

The oft-quoted slogan "When they go low, we go high" aligns with the notion of long-suffering in that we are implored and encouraged to be bigger than our enemies, critics, and detractors. We should not relinquish dignity and grace in order to enter the mud pit of our adversaries. It does not yield prosperous fruit however tempting it may be to engage in this manner. One need only spend mere moments online surveying the profane, hateful back-and-forth banter of people who spew venom at one another—and not always anonymously—via forms of social media. People attack one another personally or for their viewpoints and opinions. It is terribly disheartening to review such passive-aggressive commentary, knowing that its intent is to cause hurt and harm. Instead of succumbing to the mix, we must stay focused on personal and spiritual goals in pursuit of the truth.

Regrettably, my story is far from unique, and there are certainly many people who have struggled against greater and more enduring hardships than I. What I find fascinating about the concept of long-suffering is the spiritual opportunity it offers if we avail ourselves to it. Holding fast to personal and spiritual convictions despite persecution by others is at the core of being long-suffering. It is truly a matter of seeing the glass half full or half empty, and possessing the ability to fill the glass to the brim with lemonade made from life's lemons.

To illustrate this point, think about people who are born into challenging circumstances but overcome the obstacles of their origins. For example, in 1987, I began a career in the field of supporting people with developmental disabilities, or mental retardation as it was then known. I started out working direct care, which is attending to the personal, behavioral, and recreational needs of our clients. There were six people in all, three men and three women, ranging in age from their early fifties to seventies. They lived together in a group home which, in this case, was an old white farmhouse in a rural country setting.

These were people who, in large part, grew up isolated from mainstream society. The era in which my bookmark was created was the era in which they were born. But back then, giving birth to a child with a disability was a social disgrace. The only option available was to either shutter the "defective" child away in a secluded area of the house, such as an attic, or send the child away to an institution. There, doctors and other experts on staff were equipped to raise and train such perceived "outcasts" to contribute to the self-contained community that was the institution and its sprawling campus. Oftentimes, institutions had farms, laundries, carpentry shops and so on. The drawback is that parents were discouraged from maintaining a relationship with their child once admittance was approved. It was the proverbial Sophie's Choice of its time: to keep the child at home, endure shameful ostracization, and home school to the best of one's ability, or send them away—never to be seen again—into the hands of those who purportedly knew best.

The ugly underbelly of the institutional system is that its citizens were segregated by gender so no sexual commingling would occur. This happened, of course, but when it occurred it was often in the form of sexual abuse or rape by bigger, stronger members of one's own gender or by staff. Physical, verbal, and psychological abuse was rampant as well. Behavioral modification methods that were considered cutting edge then would be called torture now: lobotomies, food deprivation, electroshock therapy, ice baths, and physical restraints of all kinds that ranged from straitjackets to tying people to beds for extended periods of time.

One of the men in my charge was small but wiry. He was supposed to have Down syndrome but he did not have typical Down features. He spoke in a way that was almost unintelligible, though he knew exactly what he meant! (I had an unnerving dream once in which he and I had a conversation and he enunciated in perfect English throughout.) I recall that several times a year, there were times when he would wake up in the middle of the night sobbing and inconsolable. Because he didn't speak very clearly, we never knew what his nightmares were about, whether they were flashbacks of his abandoned family or traumatizing recollections of abuse perpetrated upon him. Whatever the trigger, it was obviously intense.

I eventually became the house manager and made it my mission to not only advocate for the well-being of the six house residents but to ensure that these were the most secure and contented years of their lives. And we had plenty of good times, be it playing bingo or going on picnics or singing songs from their youth. They're all gone now, but I'd like to think I contributed something positive and beneficial by transforming the way they lived their later years.

You know, in hindsight, not one of the six people for whom I was responsible ever complained about their history, their upbringing, or the lot they were dealt in life. I have great respect and admiration for those who have been long-suffering and refuse to portray themselves as victims. It would certainly be very tempting to do so, particularly if you've felt perpetually wronged and oppressed. We've all known people who play the victim card, often with an attitude of selfish entitlement. Perhaps you have a family member or acquaintance who does this. They feel they must be catered to as compensation for their suffering. Ever notice how pessimistic and toxic those people seem to be? Nothing ever suits them, not even the weather. Granted, their depression may be legitimate. But having depression is not one's fault; not doing something about it is. That's the piece within one's control. And tending to one's own wounds is what makes the difference between employing one's history to serve others instead of surrendering to one's history by destructively fueling it.

To be long-suffering does not invalidate one from being rewarded but, as is almost always the case, the rewards come when we least expect it. The rewards are simple and subtle, not accompanied by Fourth of July fireworks. They come quietly, gently in the manner of things of great importance. This is to emphasize the significance of the call that causes us to pause and take notice. If we are appreciative in our recognition, we will give thanks and express gratitude for the moment. Thus, a moment of joy is committed to memory. It can be recalled whenever need be to temper our suffering. Oftentimes, such moments are borne from an act of kindness.

Chapter 9

Kind

Kind: generous, helpful and caring about other people.
– Cambridge English Dictionary

Have you ever been waiting in line at the checkout and struck up a conversation with the person waiting in front of, or behind, you? Isn't it ironic how often we seem to have things in common with someone we have met by happenstance? In the space of a few fleeting moments, we can bond with someone who, moments earlier, was a total stranger. Perhaps part of that temporary connection included one person consoling the other by sharing their own relatable, yet similar, experience. If you are the one doing the consoling, you are in the position to be a transformative catalyst and an agent of change. And here's why: Every encounter is an exchange of energy, the best of which gets imprinted on your soul. So, when you reach out to commiserate with or comfort another, it elevates your spiritual standing as a byproduct.

In profound circumstances, that chance encounter in the checkout line can have long-lasting effect. Never underestimate the power you hold to forever alter the course of someone's life in ways that are positive and loving through a gentle smile, a kind word and a thoughtful gesture. You may find yourself standing behind someone who, unbeknownst to you, was contemplating suicide that day. But now, as a result of your interaction, that person has changed her mind. This is why it is important to compliment and praise one another when the opportunity presents itself. It is a form of support and encouragement without condescension or preaching. The checkout line stranger may now be inspired as a result of your casual observation that the color of her blouse really brings out her eyes, or that she's got a great smile. In the manner that little things mean a lot to those who are long-suffering, kindness is the key to uplifting the spirits kindred in our humanity.

Thus, kindness is to know one another in the presence of love and compassion, and to feel brotherhood toward strangers. Demonstrating kindness may manifest in generous benevolence in service to others, to be caring and compassionate for both people and animals. We may adopt a protective position with an altruistic attitude of "not on my watch." Inherently, it is the desire to protect and defend strangers as one would family. This is not to suggest that one should foster dependency for always coming to the rescue and bailing someone out. The perspective is to give someone in need a fair shake, and a lift-up or jump-start toward helping themselves.

Is responding to kindness embedded within us or is it developed and enhanced? I believe that kindness is a choice that is natural to us all. For some who have been long-suffering, it may take time to discern the authenticity of kindness. Personally, I developed kindness and compassion as a result of illuminating the truth. In the last chapter, I stated that I reacted to my abuse inauthentically. In other words, instead of taking the high road and drawing strength from my faith, I took the path that appeared to be that of least resistance. My reaction was to reciprocate the abuse but direct it at others younger and weaker than myself. None of this felt good, however, and I was filled with self-loathing.

I have come to understand that the sensation of self-loathing is intrinsic to anyone who is destructive or self-destructive. Bad acts are committed as retaliation or justification for wrongdoings perpetrated upon the actor. This brings with it a false sense of power, authority, and control, though it *never* brings happiness. Such bad actors appear to be completely devoid of a conscience. In reality, they are afraid to face the truth. Confronting the truth requires that one illuminate every corner of one's personhood and that requires vulnerability. Those who consistently deny the truth to themselves and others are incapable of this process because layers of lies must be exposed. But this is precisely the path I embarked upon to become psychic.

The time-honored adage "The truth shall set you free" is about self-healing and self-growth. I had been in denial for well over 30 years—30 years of bitterness, cynicism and mocking others to deflect attention away from myself. I made a conscious and deliberate decision to change, to transform, and to become an improved version of my old self. I came to understand that not one of us is forever locked into a pattern of behavior by which we have always been identified. It was a real-life incarnation of Ebenezer Scrooge in *A Christmas Carol*. I made efforts to reclaim the sensitivities I experienced as a child and, in so doing, I dropped my guard and allowed myself to be vulnerable. I not only confronted the truth about myself, I talked about it openly. In so doing, I found many more people responding to my gentleness than before.

I can state with honesty that kindness brings a feeling of peace and serenity regardless of age because it is fed from a divine source. Its gracious benevolence is spiritually nourished, like a running stream. There is no expiration date, no limit to the ways of kindness and our ability to access it for ourselves and others. I was 40 years old when I began my transformation and engaged with the act of becoming. So, I am living proof that it's never too late, and no one is exempt if he or she accepts the responsibility that comes with kindness.

Demonstrations of kindness are not to be committed with the expectation that it will be returned in bigger and better ways— that is simply an ego-driven inauthentic and duplicitous mindset (more about this in the next chapter). Kindness requires our loyalty to the principles of grace. Being kind is a level of consciousness that makes us mindful of how we think and behave. It is a filter for everything that passes from between our lips; a code of measurement of our thoughts; and a spiritual checklist against which to tally our actions: Is what I am doing and saying in this moment helpful, constructive, beneficial?

Being kind is to make small and large sacrifices borne out of love for one's children, significant other, and one's self. How many of us have seen news stories of very young children called to generate acts of kindness? Sometimes, these children rally the support of entire communities to fulfill a mission of kindness. It almost seems inexplicable that someone so tender in years could initiate a cause for goodness, but it happens regularly. That's the way of kindness, it begets itself. To bestow kindness upon others is not only an example of grace, it inspires hope that kindness will be reciprocated elsewhere in the form of good deeds and further kindnesses. And that is a thing of great beauty.

Chapter 10

Free From Covetousness

Covetousness: Feeling, expressing or characterized by a strong or immoderate desire for the possessions of another
— TheFreeDictionary.com

Coveting someone else's life, relationships, position, or possessions is a very dangerous prospect that can cause people to do highly irrational things. People have stolen property, destroyed marriages, and committed murder out of envy and jealousy. It seems inherent to the human condition as, from time immemorial, people can't seem to resist wanting what they lack, can't ever have, or don't want others to have. It relates back to having an attitude of entitlement for what one considers just due; people who commit bad acts out of jealousy feel justified in their motives. But to be free from covetousness is to be devoid of the envy that comes of being materialistic and egotistical.

Covetousness is purely ego driven. How many of us have wanted something—or someone—so badly and, once we achieve the desire, it's a huge disappointment or the novelty wears off quickly? It is a real-time version of the saying we may have heard our mother tell us: "Be careful of what you wish for." To be free

151

from covetousness is to dispense with the illusion that accompanies the sensation of envy. If we disavow ourselves of the entitlement attitude, we may embrace the knowledge that we have what we need—it is programmed into us. When we focus inward, we will become unconcerned with irrational wants in favor of celebrating the achievements of others. The trouble is that too many of us associate personal success with wealth.

I am not wealthy or famous and, in all honesty, I don't want to be either. I've never had an interest in money or making money for the sake of identifying as wealthy—I'm not even certain that I know for sure how much I make a year. But I know it's a lot less that what others speculate I make. The curious thing about this mindset is that I've never been without money. I've always had what I've needed and, in the times when things seemed lean, somehow, someway, money came just when I needed it. That's because it's not about money, it's about abundance.

Have you ever noticed how some of the wealthiest people in the world are the most miserable? They have every possible luxury money can buy but are emotionally bankrupt. It is the proverbial "poor little rich girl" syndrome. In recent times, there's been an emphasis on the desire to build an "empire" expediently and at all costs, such as by deception, theft, and manipulation. Inauthentic means of acquiring power and position leads to selfishness and egotistical conduct. Think about politicians, dictators, royalty, and celebrities whose behavior is seemingly without filters. They impulsively do and say whatever they please because they surround themselves with "yes" men. There's no one to tell them "no," and to inform them that their behavior is rude, insensitive or disrespectful. Deep down, we know they cannot be truly happy and contented and if they say they are, they are only fooling themselves.

Furthermore, we fuel these condescending attitudes by contributing to a societal caste system that suggests those who are rich and famous are somehow superior. The trap is set for those who then judge others based on status, wealth, appearance, or quantity of material possessions. The secret is that all of it is an illusion. It is all temporary and none of it is real in terms of our spirituality, given the context of the eons since our soul was birthed. But this attitude can be dismantled through humility.

I have always made it a point to recognize the good works of others who appear to be far less fortunate than myself. I encourage people whom I believe are doing exactly what they should be doing for their means of employment by saying, "You're really great at your job. Keep doing what you're doing!" I make it a point to tip service people where no tip is necessary or expected, and I over-tip where a gratuity is expected. You can even barter a fair and reasonable swap of goods and services without ever exchanging money. I have done this regularly, and both parties appreciate being appreciated for contributing something that is valued from one to another.

Everyone should work a service industry or manual labor job at least once in their life to appreciate how very hard some people without higher education must work to earn a living. It is a reality check for anyone who feels privileged or entitled to work alongside good folks who are tired and worn out, but persist to earn money for their family, their children or their grandchildren. Nothing dismantles a messiah complex of superiority faster than the sensitivity and concern acquired from casual interviews— where the rubber meets the road—with people who have been through the school of hard knocks.

A fact of life in this world is that we need money to survive. We need to generate an income in order to purchase goods and services basic to our essential needs. But remember this: money is a manmade concept, not a spiritual one. From a spiritual perspective, it is "real" only to the scenario of the human drama; money has no importance, no relevance, in Heaven. Therefore, ask yourself: Can I be content to live within my means? Consider how to reconcile a humble position about money from others who have financial goals as priorities. An accumulation of material goods—things—often fills an emotional void for the person acquiring them, as in a hoarding mentality. Having more money to finance more purchases doesn't address the issue, it just makes someone a wealthy hoarder.

Become unconcerned with your "have nots" for focusing on assessing your own strengths, gifts, and talents. As such, you may be poised to *earn* the things you desire in life instead of expecting them as an entitlement or pining for them unreasonably. Can you be satisfied with what you've achieved because you've worked for it and earned it, not because it was handed to you or acquired through disingenuous means? To do so is to shed old ways, childish jealousies, and petty preoccupations. To do so is a sign of spiritual maturation for shifting perceptions away from preoccupations with material possessions in favor of building spiritual and emotional capacity. To do so is to be free of covetousness.

Chapter 11

Humble

Humble: Not proud; not thinking of yourself as better than other people.
– Merriam-Webster Dictionary

To be humble is to possess the confidence for serving others and manifesting good works without the need for glory or undue adulation. That's not to suggest that one should be meek or shy. And while humility doesn't equate with being a pacifist, it does not mean we allow ourselves to be victimized either. (In other words, forgiving those who trespass against us does not equate with tolerating additional disrespectful treatment.) You may know someone who is down and out, and with very little to his or her name, but you know that same person would give you the shirt off their back if you needed it. Those same people tend to downplay their good works or decline any reward offered to them. Thus, good works can occur without glorification for doing something heroic that any decent person would do.

Embracing humility is to have the strength of character to be unconcerned about the glory of recognition. Instead, the contributions of someone who is truly humble are viewed in the context of a collaborative effort, knowing that a certain achievement was a team effort or that others influenced one's ability to succeed. Such persons shun fame, celebrity or undue attention, and exercise civility and gentility in a way that is respectful and mannerly. (Have you ever noticed how generous contributions and volunteer efforts of the rich and famous make headlines? Is this true humility?) Humble individuals are mindful of serving others with dignity, not condescension, from one peer to another and from one human being to another as well.

Being humble also requires us to defend the honor of the very gentle by considering that anyone facing great and tragic hardships could be ourselves but for the whim of fate. How often have you caught yourself thinking, "There but for the grace of God go I..." in reaction to a particularly heartbreaking incident? Humility is not occasional or situational. When we are humble, we quietly go about the business of honoring the spiritual truths that perpetually scroll in the background of our subconscious like the newsfeed ticker on a cable network. It is our conscience's essence reminding us to "keep it real" and humble. For example, I am reminded that I learned early on in my psychic work that it doesn't come *from* me, it comes *through* me. We may exert the effort, but the end result is borne of a connection with the Universe.

It is a sobering experience to go unrecognized where you feel recognition has been earned; to be treated with indifference and disregard despite one's achievements. But you cannot expect your name, reputation or accomplishments to precede you or entitle you to respect. There will always be those who do not know you, defy your principles, and yet stand firm in the validity of their own opinions and perspectives. When this occurs, it is especially important to avoid the temptation to pull rank but to, instead, listen earnestly to the other parties' questions, complaints, and positions. From this, it is hoped that all will arrive at a common understanding, or at least build together a framework from which to move forward. Just because someone is younger and inexperienced doesn't exonerate him or her from being heard and valued. And perhaps at the conclusion of a circuitous discussion, both parties can resolve to agree to disagree with civility.

The funny thing about humility is that it never allows us to rest on our laurels. This is not to suggest that we should be competitive in preserving our "status." Our good works will cause a ripple effect to occur—I've witnessed it firsthand—as we quietly yet assuredly hold influence over others, be it our children, our pupils, our co-workers, or complete strangers. This is the way of the Universe. What you bring to the world doesn't require global attention. It simply requires that you be who you are and allow your goodness to affect as many others as it is intended to. Years from now, you will be remembered for your kindnesses; perhaps not always by those still alive to recall them, but know the energy of your goodness is etched into the spiritual ethers of the afterlife.

None of us should project ourselves with an attitude of entitlement. It is a toxin. But it still stings a bit to go unacknowledged and to feel unappreciated. The older you get, the more you become aware that there's no such thing as relying on the notion that you've paid your dues. Remember how it was when you graduated from middle school to high school and felt like a little fish in a big pond? If you attended a large high school, it might've felt like a huge melting pot of kids bussed in from all over. The process of establishing yourself and making your presence known culminates with your senior year. But then, if you go on to college, military service or join the work force, it starts anew out in the real world.

To date, I've written or coauthored 20 books, including 10 autism and special needs parenting books. And I've spoken in venues across the country. However, none of it entitles me to anything. I especially understand this when I am treated indifferently or with disregard by those unaware of my work, and—most dishearteningly—particularly by the very people who are poised to create authentic change in the field of serving children, teens and adults with disabilities and their respective families. None of what I've done matters, except to those individuals for whom it has resonated. Nothing entitles me to be universally adored and embraced. Humility is the spiritual counterpoint to the "diva" attitude which is projected by many but which ultimately rings untrue and inauthentic.

If you have found yourself in the position of feeling disrespected or even ignored, it may be hard to preserve humility. Globally, it has become a struggle as the world seems to have become more violent, more divisive, and more narcissistic. But be cautioned that the age-old adage, "If you can't beat 'em, join 'em." does *not* apply. We cannot lower our standards to those of the lowest common denominator because our goal must be to aspire higher. If necessary, we must pull back and assess our approach. Perhaps we consult with others who can shed light and offer their professional, clinical or therapeutic perspective. Maybe it requires us to undergo a change and transform into someone with an enhanced grace. Perhaps we must reinvent ourselves and take stock of what we can and cannot offer the world. But we cannot sacrifice humility in the process. It is what others find gracious, mannerly, and respectable.

Chapter 12

Unselfish

Unselfish: Not selfish or greedy; generous.
– Collins English Dictionary

Many of us are often the recipients of phone calls or e-mail from worthy causes and charitable organizations soliciting monetary donations, especially at the holidays. Some of them send small "gifts" or even an enclosed coin to encourage us to reply out of duty or even guilt. The hardest to bear are the television commercials with longer-than-average run times for charities that focus on seriously ill children or animals that have been abused. This form of outreach is powerful and attention-getting but does it take the proper approach by inciting guilt in us if we do not take action by responding? I've had similar thoughts about the missionaries who go door to door in an effort to persuade me to become inducted into their membership. It feels as though they presume my spiritual beliefs are absent or could stand revision. Also, catching someone unaware at home just always seemed too intrusive to me and certainly not the way to ingratiate yourself to a stranger you hope to convert.

My point is that in the preceding instances, there's not only an implication of guilt, there's a presumption of selfishness if we do not open our pocketbook, write out a check or politely grant our patience and time. Maybe that's the key to some organizations' success, but the guilt and selfishness angle feels like an extreme and unnecessary measure to take. If we can give of our time and resources, that's great. But many of us are already making extraordinary sacrifices for our families, our communities, and other causes. A good rule of thumb to bear in mind is a modern spin on Abraham Lincoln's "You can't please all of the people all of the time..." credo. And that is, "You can't be all things to all people." As a practicing psychic, you are bound to cause dislike, disapproval, and disappointment in any number of people for being honest and forthcoming. However, you must listen to your own heart with respect to what you are called to do and give and contribute.

Being unselfish is giving when you feel *called to give* by way of donating your time and resources, as was explained earlier. It may be a matter of lending aid to those less fortunate or assuming the role of benefactor by granting wishes and making dreams come true. We all enjoy surprising others with something to cheer them and bring them happiness and joy. Doing so may require you to practice the art of sacrifice but it does not imply that you should drain your finances or run yourself ragged to appease your guilt or to suppress the notion that you are selfish.

The concept of behaving in ways that are unselfish builds upon being free of covetousness, as discussed in Chapter Ten. In the absence of want and envy, one can give freely without concern for personal or financial gain. Our vision is cleared of the illusions of our temporary existence in favor of recognizing the spiritual thrown-downs that challenge us long term or are scattered irregularly across the course of any given day. This mindset grants perspective on "selfish" versus "unselfish" because we are prompted to consider the learning opportunities which result from the choices we may make.

Being unselfish also calls us to consistently think of others and to consider others' needs as we do our own. For most of us, this is an acquired skill set. It's a curious thing that we are born egocentric. We are reliant upon adult caregivers for our every need as well as our very survival. Gradually, we grow and are taught to release that egocentricity. Early on, we learn the concept of sharing, although some of us never quite take to it. We learn the importance of collaboration and teamwork, although, again, some of us are slow learners or deliberately defy the system. And we learn that a loving, mutually respectful relationship is a reciprocal experience that asks us to make sacrifices for our loved one because it will benefit him or her. And yet, again, some of us buck convention and focus solely on how to profit from the relationship. You will probably not encounter many such folks as clients of your psychic practice because the majority will be enlightened enough to seek you out. But, rest assured, those clients will, more often that not, have selfish, manipulative family members, friends or co-workers.

Ultimately, only unhappiness can be gleaned from such a selfish mindset because it stymies our soul purpose. And our soul purpose is to take all that we know to be true of ourselves—good, bad and indifferent—and determine how best to employ it to every advantage in order to serve others. When we do this, the sacrifices we make for loved ones, as well as total strangers, require less conscious effort and are accompanied by a lessened sensation of forfeiture because we are simply doing what we *are*.

While unselfishness has become a scarce commodity, it hasn't deserted us completely nor will it ever. There will always be those people, regardless of age, who embody altruism by being pure of intention. Think of military personnel who willingly put their lives at risk so that we might enjoy freedom. Think of the call to action that occurs when natural disasters strike, and communities rally in support of both neighbors and strangers. Think of the manner in which people honor lost loved ones by holding unifying vigils. Unselfishness is a necessary component for being a good and kind and decent human being.

Unselfishness also requires setting boundaries and limits. We should not be unselfish to the point of enabling others' dependency or hemorrhaging all of our resources, including our own supply of spiritual energy. I know an older man in his seventies who has about depleted his savings trying to financially sustain his stepson. This man is a self-employed electrician whose stepson is not certified as such, but the man has employed the stepson as an electrician under his supervision. The stepson is in his early forties and has become increasingly unreliable. He can't be counted upon to show up as scheduled for a work assignment. The stepson is healthy and able-bodied but has, apparently, grown accustomed to being the beneficiary of the financial support such that he lacks all motivation except to feed his own selfishness and, I strongly suspect, his own addictions. It is a wildly unhealthy situation that is heartbreaking for the older man who believes he has been unselfish in making great sacrifices and has exhausted everything he knows to do for his stepson. But who is at fault here? The stepson who is riding his stepfather's gravy train or the man himself for not setting reasonable boundaries and limitations?

Perhaps you know a situation like this, or maybe some version of it is happening within your own family. As was noted previously, it serves no one to give away all the good bits of one's self and not leave anything behind to subsist upon. We should evaluate, on a circumstantial basis, how to use unselfishness to inspire its recipients to reclaim control over their lives. In this manner, a sense of pride and achievement may be instilled in those who will accept the invitation of help and support. There's nothing quite so satisfying as the contentment that comes of undergoing a self-initiated personal transformation. Your support is not intended to be perpetual and unending, as in the case of the electrician. Nor is it something you should be "guilted" into at the risk of creating a monstrous predicament of co-dependency that escalates and snowballs out of control. Set goals, set standards, and set expectations if someone is unable to do it for themselves. Your support is intended to be temporary, faded out as someone demonstrates that he or she is making effort to change and transform toward a self-sufficient lifestyle. The preceding philosophy absolutely has practical application in your work as a psychic because your job is to work yourself out of a job by empowering clientele and diminishing dependency.

There are, of course, exceptions to this such as parenting a child with a disability, caring for an elderly parent, or being spouse to someone whose physical or mental health is deteriorating. However, no one should be making these unselfish sacrifices in isolation because that is not healthy for the primary caregiver either. In extreme instances, the cumulative effect of the stress can trigger abuse or lead to suicide or even murder. There are service systems in place that offer options and opportunities to alleviate the pressure of feeling less than able to provide love and care to the extraordinary degree called for. It is a bittersweet form of unselfishness to acquiesce control and allow the Universe to take its course in lieu of our best efforts. It is the sacrifice of surrender.

Chapter 13

Patient

Patient: bearing provocation, annoyance, misfortune, delay, hardship, pain, etc., with fortitude and calm and without complaint, anger, or the like.
– Dictionary.com

Remember when you were very young and it seemed an eternity until school let out for summer vacation? Remember the agonizing anticipation for your birthday to come around? Like the infant programmed to be selfish only to unlearn it, so it seems that children are destined to be impatient. Like Ralphie's agonizing anticipation for his Little Orphan Annie decoder to arrive by mail in *A Christmas Story*, being patient requires self-discipline and, well, *patience*. But once we hit our twenties or so, time seems to accelerate, sometimes more quickly than we'd like. But our time is not the same as that of the Universe, which operates on an entirely different schedule.

Our culture has gradually become one of immediate gratification with minimal or no patience required. Everything, it seems, can be downloaded or communicated or ordered for delivery virtually instantaneously. This leads to *impatience* for many people accustomed to immediacy. We have been conditioned to expect instant and immediate response to our communications such that we too quickly dismiss our prayers as going unanswered when we don't receive what we want when we want it. The opportunities and experiences we are destined for will come to us, perhaps not when we want them or will them. But please know that things rarely fall into our laps without exerting effort in concert with desire. This is a point I have found myself reinforcing repeatedly with clients who are complacent in their stagnancy. Similarly, there are many times I am thankful I didn't pursue certain vocations I thought were expected of me. Because you're good at something doesn't mean you're passionate about it or that it should define who you are or what you do. This may be where patience is required as each of us finds our own way and forge our own path.

To be patient is to wait for the pupil to find the teacher, and to understand that this is a process unique to each one of us. Across our lifespan, we may, in fact, encounter any number of teachers— including those we shun and rebuke for their abuse or mistreatment of us. Patience is, then, sensing and seeing opportunities and teachable moments by accommodating timeframes that are not one's own. An example may be the fifteen-year-old girl who must weigh her options when discovering that she is expecting a baby; if she does not terminate the pregnancy, will she keep the child as her own or allow her baby to be adopted by someone who is willing to give the child the proper support? Spirit may grant insight through you for this and myriad other circumstances but be guarded for the impatient clients who press you to pinpoint a specific resolution date.

This concept of understanding patience may be more challenging for some than others who are accustomed to being impatient. For instance, I recall reading that Abraham Lincoln would never respond to an important letter impulsively but would, instead, mull his reply over the course of a day or two, so as to be mindful for both the intent and content of his communication. Thus, to be patient is to possess enough wisdom to reserve urgency for rare occasions—there are very few true emergencies in life for which we cannot wait. It is knowing that time is infinite when it comes to soul connections and intersections.

Patience is knowing that all is eventually righted in due time, although, again, it may not be according to our plan or schedule—a concept that is challenging to present to clients who are unhappy or grieving. Patience is waiting for time to take its course but disallowing the wait to become an unhealthy or irrational preoccupation, such as becoming obsessed with forcing the outcome of a situation prematurely, before it has fully come to fruition. It is akin to burning your tongue on a spoonful of hot soup without blowing on it first or allowing it to cool. Patience is a form of grace possessed by the very wise who have a history of experiences that have taught the concept—just ask a grandparent or an elderly acquaintance. Patience and wisdom walk hand in hand. Patience is contingent upon placing trust in a Higher Power. The story that follows is a fitting parable to underscore this point.

A couple of years ago, I had a psychic gallery event at a performing arts center. There were a few hundred people present and, toward the end of the evening, I opened up the floor to questions and answers by lottery drawing according to seat number. A young man's number was called—I'll call him Jason. He asked me if I could intuitively tell him anything about himself. Instead of responding directly to Jason, I began to pick up on a spiritual, grandfatherly presence around him. I described a man who had smoked, died of cancer, had a tattoo on his shoulder and had served in the military. Jason said it was his beloved grandfather. Jason added that he, too, was ex-military. With me serving as the conduit of communication, Jason's grandfather expressed concern for his impatience, particularly while driving.

He expressly called it "road rage." Jason admitted that the entire drive to the performing arts center, he was speeding and weaving in and out of traffic, cursing the whole time. Jason's grandfather told him that it was in his best interest, and that of his daughter and pregnant wife, to seek counseling and other forms of therapeutic support to work through his issues and to understand what was causing his anger. At that point, Jason confessed to having walked in a skeptic who had been mocking me up until then. He was now a believer.

A short time after all this, I received a message from Jason, thanking me and letting me know that he had taken to heart his grandfather's advice. He sought marriage counseling in addition to mental health services through the Veterans Administration. I was so pleased and proud to hear this good news. It didn't matter to me whether or not Jason believed in me personally or whether he found me credible or not. What was important is that he had acted upon the advice by taking the appropriate measures to seek out help, and was being treated for what was determined to be depression and post-traumatic stress disorder.

Amazingly, something in keeping with the theme of patience occurred as I was completing this chapter. I decided to drive in town to the post office, and, as I was backing out of my garage, I noticed something large, like an old TV antenna, spiking out of the top of the roof of my house. What the heck could that be? I pulled over to the side of the road and got a better look. There, silhouetted against the sky, was the elegant, slender outline of a blue heron. It was an amazing and unusual sight. I live in the suburbs of a popular tourist town. There's not much in the way of natural landscape that hasn't been—or isn't in the process of being—developed. Conscious that this could hold spiritual relevance, I decided to look up the heron's symbolism as soon as I got home.

In an extraordinary bit of synchronicity, a portion of the heron's symbolic meaning pertains to patience. As I discovered, the heron represents the value of being patient, holding space, and waiting for what you need to come to you. Interestingly enough, and as I have written earlier in this chapter, the heron's patience is not a passive patience of sitting back and waiting for life to happen to you. The heron symbolizes the patience that comes from taking action. In the manner that the heron is an expert fisher, we must patiently await the proper opportunities in life and then grab them and seize advantage of the moment. By doing the right thing and fulfilling our purpose, we will receive the rewards that result as the fruit of our good efforts. This was the very lesson that Jason had accepted and learned. And it is a fitting coda on which to conclude this installment of Love's Foot Rule.

Chapter 14

Pure in Thought

Purity: the quality of being unmixed, uncontaminated or wholesome.
– Yourdictionary.com

When I was growing up in the 1970s, the raciest, most forbidden thing young boys could get their hands on was *Playboy* magazine. By today's standards, Miss January's nude layout would be considered tame, even perhaps defined as art photography. As I was preparing to write this chapter on what it means to be "pure in thought," I happened upon a National Public Radio interview about the rise of the pornography industry in New York in the early 1970s. What they said was that porn was not only a multi-billion dollar industry, its burgeoning presence in our society over the past 50-plus years has directly influenced our clothes, the music we listen to, the films we watch, and even the television commercials that implore us to drink a certain beer. In fact, just today and without deliberately searching for it, I saw a reference online to Janet Jackson's infamous Super Bowl "wardrobe malfunction" many years after the fact.

To be pure in thought is especially challenging in our present age more than ever. We are inundated with others' impure thoughts imposed on us by any number of media outlets and homogenized as the new normal. By one estimate, there are an unbelievable 25 million porn sites worldwide. The top-leading site (I won't distinguish it by name) claims to receive 4.4 billion page views per month with 350 million unique visitors each month as well. Forget *Playboy*, young people of today's world are at risk of corruption from a daily assault of unsavory material of all kinds. "Sexting," and other forms of exploitation and humiliation, has elevated bullying to a level never imagined by those of us who are adults. Other contaminants come in the form of violent depictions that are emulated in real life, posted online for all to witness with disgrace and indignity.

When this book was in the process of being composed, a regrettable precedent had been set. Suddenly, a tone from the top down condones brash, insensitive behavior as "refreshingly honest." Being politically incorrect, instead of sensitive and compassionate, has seemingly been embraced by the very people who should be raising the bar and upholding the standards for diplomacy and civil temperament. Instead, racism, misogyny and hateful rhetoric is excused, downplayed or defended as "speaking one's mind" or "punching back." The danger is that others emulate what they see and hear, causing tremendous division among our population. With the advent of the internet, this is far-reaching and insidious as well as anonymous.

So much about the way people communicate with one another seems impersonal any more. I take long daily walks and have noticed people who don't look up to acknowledge me as we cross paths for talking or texting on their phone. Sometimes, the rare person not using a cell phone doesn't look up to say "hello" either. I don't think it's because I'm unapproachable either; I always make a point to make eye contact and smile. A lot about the way people communicate also seems very passive-aggressive. That is, by communicating remotely and over the internet, someone can preserve his or her anonymity and say or post the most impure things! Take a look at comments people make on any online social media or news forum that permits reader commentary. Unless someone is moderating carefully to delete hurtful messages, a lot of really abusive things get said—things that are unlikely to be said publicly, face to face. But under the cover of remote communication, it's become a veritable free for all. And that's not healthy, nor is it a good thing. Personally, I find it cowardly.

The trouble with this kind of behavior is that it becomes a corrosive cancer. I have known very sneaky, very destructive people who readily defend and justify their motives for what others perceive as bad behavior. These are people who are terribly unhealthy, not just mentally but physically as well. You see, your mental-emotional state cannot help but to affect your physical well-being. Eventually the ugliness of the verbal abuse and scheming ways sets up shop physically, manifesting in any number of chronic ailments that usually give the sufferer another reason to complain. These are the people who are frequently sick—and loudly lament so all others know. Their immune system is compromised and they are highly susceptible to illnesses. They may develop immune deficiency-type illnesses, or even cancer, because the hate has manifested in real time, in physical form. You will witness this in your psychic work, if you haven't already, when it comes time to discuss a client's spouse, in-law, parent, sibling, or even their own child.

Most significantly, those who are of impure thought or seemingly without conscience never seem to grow, to mature or evolve. When I think of the people who have deliberately gone out of their way to derail me through devious, deceptive means over the years, I think of people that I now see as pathetic for having their spiritual growth stunted. They'll whine and whimper and point the finger of accusation at anyone but themselves. But they have never changed, even over the course of several decades, and I find that sad. One person, in particular, is a serial sexual predator who has harassed and made unwanted advances against others for decades, and yet this person has somehow brainwashed a certain constituency into overlooking his bad behavior. But, just like what happened to actor Kevin Spacey, television anchor Matt Lauer, and mogul Harvey Weinstein, truth and purity will one day prevail. In the interim, this person's outward appearance reflects his manipulative, predatory habit of using others before discarding them. He has aged beyond his years, burdened with the weight of his crimes.

Being pure in thought is not only about making efforts to resist the distractions of corruption. To be pure in thought is to set firm boundaries by disallowing negative thoughts from intruding upon, and interrupting, one's quality of life. (These negative mental interruptions that cause you to doubt yourself and your psychic abilities are the single greatest hinderance to your success.) In the past, I found that associating with certain people or certain groups was toxic and, wanting to rise above it all, I simply walked away and never looked back. I don't miss the cliques, the judgmental cynicism, or the attitude of superiority. This extends to family members too. It is important to call out those thoughts that seek to tempt and seduce us with the realization of their destructive potential.

Oftentimes, we don't even notice how our thinking has been affected by certain people around us because our own thought processes are so fractured. For example, I know of a family so steeped in a culture of dysfunction that they tried to minimize and defend a family member who was arrested (and later charged and incarcerated) for pedophilia. Outside of that circle, the offense is crystal-clear; within the culture of dysfunction, the collective vision has become muddied in a skewed version of normalcy and excuse-making rationalizations. Be prepared to encounter similar such situations in your psychic work, and decide how to temper the truth about those who are not pure in thought in ways that will be sensitively communicated by yourself and gratefully received by your clients.

You may already know people who are perpetually cynical and pessimistic, always commenting and complaining with bitterness and sarcasm. They are quick to portray themselves as victims and—more often than not—are the instigators of their own drama. Most of us know someone like this, but have you ever paid careful attention to what goes on within their energy field? They bemoan the cloud hanging over them because there really *is* a cloud hanging over them—it's a cloud radioactive with counterproductive energy! These are the people for whom everything goes wrong, or so it would seem. These are the people for whom every device, every appliance, malfunctions in their hands even though the same item worked perfectly just before or after for someone else. Computers crash, televisions and cell phones scramble, and coffee makers die. Have you noticed this? It's a remarkable phenomenon that grants credibility to the notion that you get back what you put out.

For some of us, being in the presence of those who are of impure thought, who are self-serving, and who are destructive, is unavoidable. If you find this to be the case, spiritual protection is essential. What I have found to be useful is a technique that also requires conscious and deliberate effort. It is simplistic but it is not "once and done." It requires regular, mindful thought to reinforce its purpose. When you know you are going to be in the company of negative-thinking people, close your eyes, take three deep breaths, and imagine a glorious, golden veil of light wafting down around you from above. It is translucent like a cobweb but as impenetrable as steel. Picture the shimmering veil gently covering your head and shoulders like a hooded cape as it descends downward to wrap you in its protective shield from head to toe. You may be surprised at the nonreaction you receive from the complainers and the pessimists who give you a wide berth or ignore being near you altogether. In the best-case scenario, your veil of protection may actually prompt these folks to say something helpful and positive!

Personally, in addressing your own needs, it is important to set boundaries and limitations from intrusive thoughts. We all periodically have negative thoughts that are primarily our own anxiety processing what happened in the past or venting over what's coming in the future. For some, negative thoughts are self-effacing and self-deprecating. These kinds of thoughts may be psychological residue from hardships or abuses previously endured, perhaps stemming from post-traumatic stress disorder. Harmful thoughts may become intrusive, giving rise to instability and affecting the quality of our everyday lives. What's alarming is when the thoughts become not only intrusive but instructional, telling us to harm ourselves or others. You may have even "heard" these commands in a voice other than the one you use to talk yourself through something situational.

If this is the case, it is urgent that you take charge and shut down anything negative that dominates and repeatedly loops in your mind. You are in control; your thoughts are just thoughts, and they do not define or control you. Also, be mindful of what you allow yourself to be exposed to in terms of outside influences, viewing material, and the previously mentioned toxic personalities. To be pure in thought is to be unfettered by such deceptive energies that seek only to defame and derail us in a grand scheme of temptation. This is an illusion of the mind.

The challenge is to create a personal balance between what you believe and what you get exposed to. Prolonged exposure leads to imbalance and this can translate to insensitive treatment of others. To reverse this effect, it is necessary to reflect, through words and good deeds, the essence of one's inner self, like peeling away layers of an onion in order to illuminate the truth. This is the procedure for uncovering an ethical balance between human temptation and spiritual motivation. For some, it is moment by moment. When we are gracious and transparent in words and actions, and behave no differently in public or private, we are endeavoring purity of thought.

Chapter 15

Truth-Loving

Truth: An idea of "truth to self," or authenticity.
— Wikipedia.com

The last chapter concluded with a discussion about the importance of being pure in thought by illuminating the truth. To be truth-loving is to embrace the liberation that accompanies the lightness of truth. To be unafraid of illuminating the truth is having nothing to hide and no secrets to reveal. No spiritual or emotional blackmail can occur when one is wholly transparent. But this also requires total honesty with ourselves about ourselves. This is a process for each of us that takes into account where we've been, where we are, and where we're going. This informs our perspective of truth for learning from past successes and mistakes as we advance. It is an effort to justify one's innate desire for decency and goodness by embracing the truth and eradicating deception. To live in truth is to be emboldened to call out untruths. Transparency grants perspective because we have confronted the truth about ourselves, good, bad, and indifferent. A skill set develops in which we embody a tendency to deflect and repel

179

untruths. This is the beauty of transparency, which is a hallmark of your psychic practice.

When I think about this kind of transformation—walking in truth—I think of Owen. Owen and I have never actually met in person, but we were introduced to one another over the radio. I was being interviewed on a live call-in show about my psychic work and, in particular, the potential for negative, harmful energies to prey upon those of us who are weak or vulnerable. Toward the end of the program, a gentleman phoned in to speak with me. I'll never forget the way he introduced himself: "My name is Owen and I'm a heroin addict." I was overwhelmed. The show's hosts wanted to keep things moving and, I sensed, perhaps weren't taking Owen too seriously. But I made a point of pausing to underscore what had just happened. I thanked Owen for his honesty, and told him that what he did in that moment, live and on-air within earshot of untold listeners, was incredibly brave and important. As referenced in the prior chapter, Owen was grappling with destructive thoughts that were influencing him to harm himself and others. I suppose any number of people struggling with addiction feel as he did. I wanted to be certain that I had a way to connect with Owen after the show and the hosts were good enough to get his phone number to me. I cannot resist holding great respect and empathy for anyone who so humbles himself by stating, upfront, "this is my challenge in life." He wasn't asking for pity or a handout, he just wanted to be heard.

When I was able to connect with Owen, he was grateful that I followed up with him. However, he was really hurting and in a bad way. He was a middle-aged man sleeping on his mother's sofa and she had given him an ultimatum to get out. He couldn't hold a job. He lost custody of his two sons. And, he told me, that after we were finished talking, he was probably going to go rob someone to get enough money for a fix. For some reason, perhaps legitimate, perhaps not, he was ineligible for a bed in a halfway house or there were no beds available. I felt as though he had no one to talk to who really cared as he poured out his story.

At a young age, he had been raped repeatedly by men who were older and more powerful. The shame, humiliation, and embarrassment caused a downward spiral in his life that led to petty crime which led to incarcerations. As I expected, Owen said drugs helped numb the pain. Like a dog chasing its tail, the drugs also led to a self-fulfilling prophecy of suicidal thoughts and collusion with shady acquaintances who were never really friends. These people only portended their allyship so long as he had cash to pay for drugs; when he was broke and begging for a fix, they could've cared less and cut him off, as he later confessed. Before long, very dark energy began to take hold over his life and he was hearing manipulative voices. Owen also began to see black, shadow-like shapes that further distorted his ability to distinguish the truth. His rock bottom came when he was denied visitation with his boys. Owen said being in prison helped him to dry out but also gave him time to reflect and craft a plan.

I spoke with Owen again recently. He was facing another arrest for an unpaid fine and had only two hours to raise twenty-five dollars or be incarcerated again. I wasn't sure whether I could fully believe him, but he did affirm that his worst day sober was better than his best day as an addict. I told him I would say a prayer that he would be granted a spiritual stay through some divine intervention and avoid jail. At his core, Owen means well and is, I believe, a decent human being struggling to reconcile the past. But I give him credit for his transparency in being truth-loving. Regrettably, his case has become commonplace in the midst of the opioid epidemic.

When I consider the concept of truth-loving on a personal level, I think about my own transformation, as I previously shared. I have to believe that part of being truth-loving is about the company we keep. I can recall that during the most challenging period of my life, I was surrounded by people of questionable character. Like Owen's so-called accomplices, these were individuals who lied and betrayed others, who had a weak moral compass, and who were rather self-centered to say the least. One person brought an insect to a restaurant, tucked in her purse. After eating a big dinner, she put the bug on her plate, mixed it into her leftovers and complained about it to the management in order to get a free meal. Another person—a supervisor, actually—really set a tone of insensitivity toward others that I found myself emulating, although I wasn't fully aware of it at the time.

Now that I have liberated myself from an inauthentic façade by confronting the truth in tandem with putting forth effort to change for the better, I am surrounded by people with higher qualitative standards. It really is astounding to reflect on this in hindsight and see how we really do tend to attract to us energies that are similar or on par with that of our own. As you might have intuited in your own psychic readings, this may be why the woman who was abused as a child continually attracts the same men who both are alcoholic and physically violent. Maybe this is the reason that people who always seem to be chronically ill or depressed attract others of the same mindset. In essence, like attracts like. Perhaps you've even witnessed this within your own family. How many times does someone cry "wolf" for loaning the wrong "friend" money or committing the same mistakes by "taking back" someone who has used him or her repeatedly. In each instance, the company kept is clearly seen as bad news to everyone except the person who wears blinders and refuses to admit the truth.

Further, when we are truth-loving, there is no evading authenticity because it is a way of life, not something we must stop and think about as it applies to the present circumstances. It is not a mindset, it is a lifestyle. Our heightened intuition will work to our advantage in challenging situations when we require the proper words to use, or direction on taking action that is most altruistic. It is a great and satisfying feeling to know that our spiritual allies are truth-loving as well; they can best collaborate in concert with us when we live and abide by the truth. When this occurs, the rhythm of spiritual energy as it aligns with our own is nearly palpable, almost tangible. It manifests in a series of signals and synchronicities that unfold across each day. Our recognition of these guideposts aligns with our heightened awareness as a practicing psychic. It is then that we know we are walking in the truth of our destined design, and are fulfilling our purpose in life.

Chapter 16

Endurance

Endurance: The power to withstand hardships and stress.
— Definitions.net

As was previously mentioned, to embrace the ideals of a truth-loving existence, one must not only project altruistic ideologies, one must exist by the tenets of goodness. Again, this is not merely a situational mindset, it is a whole-life approach that requires consistent mindfulness and discipline to achieve and maintain. Thus, endurance is to *sustain* by adhering to fundamental beliefs of goodness and truth. When this occurs, what we contribute becomes timeless and classic for the sound, basic wisdom that is valued by countless others. This results in glowing word of mouth and repeat business for your psychic work as more and more people are called to you. When essential good thoughts and altruistic deeds are valued globally, it elevates our collective way of being with one another as a human race—and that's a heady responsibility if you feel appointed to do so beginning within your own community. A committed dedication burgeons across time for knowing our existence is a spiritual collaboration, united with those who share the same core mores of charity, compassion, love, and truth.

But endurance may be both a collective experience as well as a personal and individualized process. The stamina of one's endurance is determined by a combination of faith and physiology. Faith, itself, need not be construed as religious or spiritual. Faith may be an internal devotion to the preservation of self—a drive to honor one's abilities and attributes so that one will endure, if not succeed. It is a testament to the space we each occupy in the world, to leave our mark knowing we have made a contribution of lasting value.

Our individual physiology makes endurance a delicate dance when faith is wavering or tested. Our senses can be bombarded, assaulted every day. We may become distracted, derailed by a collision of undermining circumstances and negative personalities. This can be as debilitating as it is draining. Our energy is sapped, and our physical and mental-emotional well-being is significantly compromised. Efforts to recover and recoup may make endurance challenging. Merely subsisting is a seemingly insurmountable labor. In brief, some of us are simply too sensitive for this world.

My youngest brother was one such person. His birth was complicated by oxygen deprivation, though he was spared the intellectual impairment we were cautioned was a possibility. As a child, he was flaxen-haired and fair-skinned. With three very diverse older brothers, he was well-rounded for having had so many influences. But as he grew into adolescence and adulthood, he would define himself as a social outlier. He felt awkward and moody, excluded from lasting friendships and "buddy" cliques. He desperately desired romance but was duped out of thousands of dollars by a "mail order" girlfriend who professed her love and absconded with an expensive engagement ring, never to be heard from again. His increasing bouts with depression made steady employment difficult, and he became dependent on a combination of prescription medication and alcohol to cope. He eventually became unreachable, abandoning his filthy apartment and isolating himself in the home of a brother who was his self-appointed caretaker.

He spoke about, threatened or attempted suicide on any number of occasions but repeatedly refused clinical hospitalization. One night when things seemed particularly hopeless, he transcribed his goodbye notes and overdosed on pills and liquor. It is some consolation that he slipped away peacefully and of his own design, no longer burdened by the mortal troubles that plagued him. Or, as he put it, "I was doomed from the start." He had lost the will to go forward and couldn't foresee a logical rationale for doing so. One might question the endurance of my brother and countless others like him. It's not that he couldn't endure, it's that he endured as long as he could.

The preceding contention should not be mistaken for advocating suicide. That life is precious is a cliché, though one founded in truth. But life is not a "one size fits all" prospect. We manage to the best of our ability based on our personal resilience, our support system, and the currency of love that finances our endurance. When those aspects of sustenance seem irretrievably depleted, it makes surrender seem irresistibly attractive. Have you ever felt invisible? Have you ever wanted to give up? If so, perhaps you are best poised to understand.

I have been invisible on any number of occasions. In each of them, I was attempting to function and assimilate within a broken system. Because my insights and perspectives are considered unique by some, I have served as a consultant to several different organizations. Though I was initially revered in each instance, the luster eventually grew tarnished when my overtures for change and transformation went unheeded. You see, when people inhabit a culture of dysfunction, it is akin to the classic adage of not holding vision enough to see the trees for standing in the forest. The myopathy becomes the local version of normal despite an outsider objecting to the apparent and obvious dysfunction. A rigid and unyielding mindset impedes the ability to endure for being inauthentic.

In each instance, a tyranny reigned—one or two individuals at the top who were driven by ego and closed to (or threatened by) change. The culture of dysfunction generated myriad weaknesses in the mental-emotional, physical, and spiritual well-being of those involved. People were literally sick but portrayed themselves as victims in an effort to justify their refusal to evolve. Yet, in each instance change came regardless of my participation or the protest of some. Those who were able to be open to it, suitably adapted for having donned new lenses. Still others were compelled to change due to pushback from those who also objected to the dysfunction, despite pleas of denial to the contrary.

Endurance is a means of working through struggles by reverting to one's basic principles of goodness. Endurance does not surrender to the "if you can't beat 'em, join 'em" mindset. It is a conviction to defend the truth. Thus, there is no greater accomplishment than to stand in the light of uncompromising truth. When this occurs, we are better able to put forth the effort necessary to manifest dreams, free from inauthentic distractions. Endurance need not be all-consuming and overwhelming; it may be as simple as practicing decency and common courtesy. These principles are timeless because they appeal to our inherent kindness. We must defend these principles from those who do not practice them. We cannot fight fire with fire except under extraordinary circumstances and as a last resort. Instead, we need to look for teachable moments and persuasive learning opportunities. Remember: the wise teacher does not provide all the answers but leads the pupil to discover the answers in his or her own time. It will serve your clients well if you support them to consider your intuitive guidance while they arrive at a plan of resolve on their own.

Of course, it is love that is the underlying motivator that grants impetus to endurance. I think of people I have known for whom this is true. My grandmother who was married for 30 years, became a widow and never remarried—nor had the desire to—but kept going for over 40 years more by devoting herself to friends, family and the community. She knew she was needed by those who loved her, and that propelled her endurance.

I also think of the countless families of people with autism I have known. I have been in many homes, from those who were affluent to very modest, rural abodes that were little more than shacks with dirt floors. But where love reigned, nothing else mattered. It was love within the family united that sustained the endurance of each family against a service system that presumed to know best and was often driven more by bureaucracy than by compassion.

I consider those individuals who have grappled with addiction to illegal substances, alcohol or prescription medication. These folks are usually attempting to assuage emotional trauma by self-medicating to suppress the psychological damage. This damage usually harkens back to emotional neglect, physical or sexual abuse. Oftentimes, men like Owen are ashamed and embarrassed to confess the extent and degree of the horrors they suffered, tending to minimize their experiences by brushing them off, or refusing to discuss them at all. Where healing has occurred, it is because love was the conduit that granted a gradual recovery of self.

There are times in our lives when our ability to endure is impeded by any number of circumstances including physical ailments and emotional setbacks. We may seem as though we are spinning our wheels, not gaining any traction, when – wham! – you're dealt another blow by coming down with an illness or serious malady. It seems in that moment that the odds are working against you. But, by an unconventional and spiritual irony, it has been my experience that this is the time when things are designed to reset and reboot us. You may indeed have been stuck in a holding pattern, feeling hopeless and probably attracting like-minded people and negative energy to you.

One of the least harmful options available to our spiritual allies is to sidetrack us temporarily in order to initiate a reconstruction. So, what appears to be more bad luck may actually be a blessing in disguise. Such a spiritual "time-out" is an opportunity to reflect, self-examine, and reassess our priorities. It is a chance to tend to self-care without overextending ourselves into the old way of trying to be all things to all people. We are compelled to accept the setback as compensation for the reconstruction and allow for it, because the circumstances are out of our control. We simply must let things take their course and play out. But know that it is the care and concern of our spiritual allies that makes this unusual paradigm possible.

So, you see, sometimes an illness is the only way that Spirit can contain you long enough to tune-up and realign your energy, though it may seem totally unfair in the moment. For some people, "bad luck" seems to be a common occurrence, almost as if it replays on a continuous loop; but consider how those same individuals approach their obstacles. Are they chronic complainers who play the victim card and never seem to heed the wake-up call? Or do they accept the obstacles as a challenge to meet and rise above? You could certainly identify any number of people you've encountered who have seemingly been dealt unfair odds and have overcome their struggles to survive. In each instance, it was more than perseverance that fueled their endurance, it was the love of others who cared, and were concerned and committed to support their success. It was also a love and belief of self that contributed to the longevity of those who have endured.

Chapter 17

Faith

Faith: A strong belief in a supernatural power or powers that control human destiny.
– Vocabulary.com

Faith is a belief system that is both personal and spiritual. It goes without saying that faith is the backbone of our humanity. If we were collectively without faith, we would be entirely ego-centric, cynical, and spiritually void. Faith propels us forward with both optimism and valor. There is an inherent trust that we have been placed here with a purpose to teach, bless, and heal one another under the auspices of the unseen love that unites us as one. By bringing others to this collaborative ideology, we may strengthen faith's conviction in numbers.

There's truth to the wise adage that suggests even if you don't believe in God, God believes in you. This is because faith is a component of the soul that connects us to a Higher Power and assures us that we will be all right. Thus, the crux of Spirit is a constant in our lives, evidenced by the emotion we experience when we give and receive love, or by the way in which we strive to persevere and overcome the obstacles before us, as was discussed in the preceding chapter. Like most relationships, the one we share with Spirit is a reciprocal relationship, meaning that we are most likely to recognize how Spirit manifests outward expressions of divine presence the more we are conscious of Spirit's essence. If we are attentive, this displays in a variety of "alignments" or synchronicities that provide us with guideposts, or validations, or answers to questions throughout each day, as you have likely noticed in your psychic growth.

Such instances are examples of "entrainment," in which our heart and mind rhythmically align both internally and with that of others. When it occurs internally, we are more susceptible to interpreting the synchronicity of looking up at the digital clock and seeing it read 1:11 or 3:33. (Many of you reading this just had an Aha! moment for witnessing triple digits as often as you are.) We may more carefully consider the majestic hues of a glorious sunset. And we may be prone to recalling profound dreams that seem to hold meaning for being so vivid and lucid. When entrainment happens between us and another party, it may manifest in a moment of shared inspiration or problem-solving, such as a creative solution to a struggle that satisfies all parties. Shared entrainment is also the experience of spontaneously laughing or crying with someone with whom we share a close bond in reaction to something felt but unheard and unseen.

When we experience entrainment with Spirit, we may feel divinely guided as if we are receiving direction from a caring mentor, a brotherly force, or a glorified version of our own conscience. We may make better or more informed choices. We may be impressed with words of wisdom and an even temperament. We may experience the sensation of a blissful serenity where others are sarcastic and pessimistic. But, like any relationship, one must be demonstrative, conscious and aware of contributing to it, otherwise we risk being defined as a fair-weather friend—someone who's only there when you need them. You would quickly shun a one-sided relationship with someone who only contacts you when they want something, wouldn't you? The most satisfying relationships are those in which both parties are attuned to the wants and needs of one another; and are actively engaged in building and strengthening the union. The same may be said for the relationship with Spirit. Who would be better attuned to our wants and needs than the originator of our very creation?

But when the relationship with Spirit is neglected, then it becomes a relationship of convenience. Some cynics behave as if Spirit is Santa Claus, only thought about on rare occasion or in cases of dire emergency—except usually then it is to ask for something, perhaps selfishly or superficially. Depending upon the degree of desperation, such individuals will offer Spirit or God or the Universe a bargain; they consent to change their behavior if Spirit will do something in exchange. Under these circumstances, is it reasonable to expect instantaneous results in answer to prayers? It's much like calling up a former classmate you haven't had contact with since high school and asking to borrow money—you know it's awkward and uncomfortable, but you humble yourself regardless in hopes of a merciful outcome. Chances are you would be dismissed, or the other person would make excuses to rebuff you.

But when we frequently express appreciation, gratitude, and thanksgiving, we are honoring our relationship with Spirit and strengthening the direct line of communication we share. We are simultaneously building a spiritual reserve within ourselves from which to draw upon as needed for strength and resiliency. Think of it like making deposits into a bank savings account. You are contributing something of value for safekeeping on a regular basis, knowing it will accrue interest, and confident that you can draw against the spiritual reserve when necessary. This is not to say that any one of us is more deserving of a spiritual presence in our lives. But treasuring an awareness for the constancy of the relationship with Spirit makes some us of feel as if we are opening little gifts on a regular basis, instead of complaining about getting stuck with a lump of coal for not having our prayers answered on-demand.

Faith is a wholehearted belief that goodness will prevail, given the unification of many individuals making deposits into a collective spiritual reserve. You see, because we are all more alike than different, faith is both personal as well as it is universal. Our daily output of optimism, and kind and gracious conduct, contributes to the community pot that is accessible to us all. That is why some people feel enlightenment for participating in religious or spiritual ceremonies; or they experience the unification of strength in numbers at a prayer vigil. It is because the opportunity to come together as one is a validation of our collective humanity—evidence for the very best of what we share in common as human beings.

It was having faith that allowed me to press onward in my darkest hour. I remember being sixteen, and home by myself. The rest of my family was on an outing that I declined in my miserable desire to simply be left alone. So deep was my depression during that period that I sat for some time, holding my father's old straight razor, contemplating an act of self-harm. I mentally imagined what it would feel like to draw the blade across my wrist. Would I panic at the first sight of blood, or would I register relief for the impending closure to my suffering? If I could muster enough courage to follow through, I also imagined that I would become immune to my own self destruction. I would be overcome by lightheadedness and a ringing in my ears that would grow increasingly louder until I gave myself permission to enter the safety of the sound and disappear forever.

Yet my suicidal thoughts were prevented by a voice. It wasn't something externally audible, but the traditional small, still voice from within that we have heard referenced in spiritual teachings. And the voice said, "No, no. Don't do this thing. One day people will know who you are for what it is that you have to offer them." At that moment in time, I had absolutely no idea what that meant, or what that would look like. But it was enough to dissuade me from piercing my flesh and hemorrhaging into oblivion. I was possessed of a new understanding. Knowing that I was the keeper of something valuable, for which I'd be recognized someday, made me feel as though I had been singled out, selected for some purpose beyond my present comprehension. It didn't make my suffering any easier, but it did make it more bearable knowing that what I was enduring was ultimately a temporary derailment until better conditions manifested. And they did.

If I had been totally devoid of faith, I probably would not be writing these words for having taken my own life. Let me be clear as well: I'm not talking about faith in God or Spirit or a Higher Power necessarily. At that time, I was indifferent and thoughtless when it came to the notion of God. I was one of those cynical fair-weather friends, thinking God owed me. The faith I'm speaking of is a faith that our lives are dynamic, that things will improve, and that something greater can await us if we believe it to be so. This may call for reliance on a paternal Higher Power for comfort. I did eventually re-establish my relationship with God. God had never abandoned me, as I would learn, despite my having all but abandoned God. It is our birthright as human beings to exercise our faith in personal spirituality.

With that relationship now reclaimed, I am certainly living proof of faith on another level of connectivity, being my work as a psychic medium. But it was not an overnight process. As you will read in the next chapter, I put my faith in an unseen but loving and benevolent force, one that wishes for us each to succeed by fulfilling our destiny. With that faith came an understanding about the mechanics of spiritual communication and a path of new direction for myself. It was a wonderful healing and reawakening process. Or, as is popular to say nowadays, I got "woke."

Chapter 18

Hope

Hope: To want and expect something to happen or be true.
— MacMillan Dictionary

Hope is a belief in the promise that the will of spiritual goodness will persevere. In its purest form it is the spirit of optimism; a resolve dedicated to good efforts and good works. The driving desire is that collective hope will create positive outcomes. Hope is Faith's twin sister, inextricably intertwined and incomplete absent the other. This is because hope is the universal plea of mercy as well as the projection of our longings, which is most often accompanied by faith. Hope fuels our dreams, desires, and expectations when we choose to elect optimism as a matter of course.

It is a common belief among all human beings to desire the best and to impress our longing with every expectation that good things will prevail. We need to believe that our spiritual allies and supporters desire us to be successful. For centuries, people have prophesized an end of days that never came. There have surely been instances when it seemed close to occurring given the plagues, natural disasters, and wars in the history of the world. But would a Higher Power really permit us to destroy ourselves? In its purest sense, hope is the desire that our wishes and intentions will align with the Universe's plan for us, believing that prayers truly are answered. Hope is a form of solace in knowing that the burden of what is to come is not solely our own. This was the mindset I adopted in order to instigate a significant change in my own life's trajectory.

I had reached a point in my life in which I was becoming more self-aware than ever before. I was not only rediscovering and reclaiming my personal spirituality, I was learning things previously unknown about aspects of my very personhood. As I stated earlier, since 1987, I have been employed and involved in the field of providing services for people with developmental disabilities and, particularly, autism. Autism remains a greatly misunderstood neurological experience that many still equate with intellectual deficiency rather than a more sensitive, unique way of perceiving the world. By 1994, I had progressed to the level of being employed in the government office that developed and oversaw policy for these citizens statewide.

Imagine my surprise to experience a spiritual awakening simultaneously with an existential awakening. I'm relating this here because this was a period of time in my life that was full of hope for my future aspirations. Prior to then, I had only known autism in a stereotypical sense. I had only previously encountered individuals who did not speak, or who made indistinguishable vocalizations; and who rocked their body, flapped their hands, and seemed to overreact to loud noises such as crowds or even fireworks. But the more I became embroiled in meeting autistic self-advocates—individuals with autism who were able to openly express their wants and needs—the more I felt a kinship.

One day, I explained this kinship to a friend of mine, a young woman with autism. Her response was to suggest that I consider Asperger's syndrome, a diagnosis which, at the time, was something of a milder "cousin" to the symptomology of classic autism. As I reviewed the symptoms, it felt like fitting into place jigsaw puzzle pieces that, until that moment, had been fragmented, random and scattered. Now a complete and logical scenario was made whole. Aspects of my life that had been concerning or perplexing—such as my lifelong inability to assimilate socially—made total sense. And as relieving as it was to have an explanation for my way of being in the world dating back to my earliest childhood memories, it also presented another hurdle if I was to be thoroughly transparent.

My next challenge was what to do with the new information about my self-revelation. I had to sift and sort and figure out how to "own" it entirely. This was both humbling and daunting. It was very much a coming out process to reveal this previously dormant component of my personhood and make it public. The specter of the label loomed large before me. Like someone who realizes and comes to terms with their own sexuality, could I befriend the label and make peace with it? Or would I continue to keep it at bay by suppressing my very identity instead of embracing it?

When we consider people who are different from how we see ourselves, we have often been conditioned to not only perceive ourselves as superior but to also justly judge and criticize them. This perception of "us" and "them" gives rise to a culture of fear. The culture of fear grants permission for those who subscribe to it to actively project this belief system upon others as "correct" or "true." This attitude may lead to misogyny and racism as well as a slew of "phobias," such as xenophobia or homophobia. However, therein lies the secret: the culture of fear is not a fear of our differences, it is a fear of confronting our mutual similarities. We are all more alike than we are different; but how many among us can illuminate the truth about our own faults, frailties or imperfections? How many of us are willing to publicly peel away the emotional layers that cloak us in favor of liberating us all as one human race?

It is sometimes simply easier not to enter a period of self-examination and self-assessment in deference to the same-old-same-old. But we may also reach a point at which we become sick and tired of feeling sick and tired—and, under the proper conditions, this grants us incentive to transform. In order to grow and to hold hope for one's future evolution, personal change is a necessary process. Not one of us is locked into portraying ourselves as others have always known us to be, even if that personality has been cynical, judgmental, and unhealthy. We can transform at any given moment. By so doing, we may dismantle the culture of fear for setting an example. We may become beautifully transparent in confessing our trespasses, atoning for any harm we have caused in the past, and owning our story with truth and candor.

If you have grown up confused or frightened by your own psychic abilities, or haunted by experiences you struggled to explain, perhaps you understand a similar coming-to-terms process. There is no one else who has experienced all that you have; your life is uniquely your own. Be unafraid and unashamed to tell your story, good, bad, and indifferent. Allow hope for becoming an improved version of your old self to serve as the motivation that grants authenticity to your purpose. You may be surprised at how your new identity draws others, who will learn and heal from its inspiration, and attracts those with a similar story to tell. Perhaps you will find this approach as richly satisfying as I have.

Chapter 19

Unfailing

Unfailing: Constant; unflagging: unfailing loyalty.
– The American Heritage Dictionary of the English Language

The twelfth and final tenet of Love's Foot Rule is unfailing. When we think about unfailing as a concept, certain, old adages may come to mind, such as "Practice makes perfect," "Persistence pays off," or even "Pick yourself up, dust yourself off, and start all over again." If perseverance leads to deliverance, we may define unfailing as a dedication, devotion, and loyalty to uphold one's belief system, steadfast in believing that the truth will be illuminated. When we are unyielding in our determination to honor the truth and to conduct ourselves with propriety, we simultaneously, gently, and heroically uphold the truth as a beacon for others while confounding disbelieving critics and cynics. If all prior tenets are in alignment, all should be in perspective, putting energy into proper placement. Thus, unfailing is a blend of personal and spiritual commitment to contribute good and valuable things to the world.

This is an ideal but, in reality, the world hurts and being human is hard work. Every day we are challenged with strife and unrest politically, spiritually, physically, and mentally. Yet, at some point in our soul's trajectory, we opted to incarnate in human form, knowing we were signing up for the potential struggles that can so readily be a byproduct of inhabiting that human form. But with such a colorful and broadly diverse mix of personalities, it is certainly very challenging at times to balance protecting ourselves with tending to the needs of others.

Do you know people who thrive on creating soap-opera drama where none existed? Do you know someone who is consistently sarcastic, cynical, and judgmental? Have you encountered those who are self-centered and ego-driven, caring only for gratifying their selfish needs for lust, greed or power? How about the folks who never take personal responsibility for their own mistakes or inactions, always pointing the finger of blame at others while making themselves out to be the victim? Rest assured that if you are reading this book, you are most definitely not one of them, because none of them would give reading this book a second thought. But you *are* reading this book, which in and of itself is a communication that you desire to be unlike individuals with such low-vibration attributes and aspirations. Instead, you wish to make serviceable your most profound psychic gifts.

Still, it may also seem that life is unfair, or that good fortune is not evenly distributed for those same individuals appearing to succeed on bad behavior or get by on playing the victim card in perpetuity. We may feel "Why bother?" or "What's the use?' when we witness others who seem to be rewarded for their misconduct, granting credence to the old saying, "Nice guys finish last." It may appear as though those who slide by on bad behavior are "winning," but there's a little something called *karma* to which they are usually completely oblivious.

In essence, the stereotypic perception of karma is that you get back what you put out, and "what goes around, comes around."

This implies that karma is a spiritual form of comeuppance or punishment, and it can come across that way if we're not paying attention. But karma is supposed to be interpreted as a learning opportunity and a teachable moment. Think about it: Do people who behave badly and consistently mistreat others "win" forever? At some point, there's got to be a shift to account for spiritual compensation—a wake-up call, if you will. Sometimes, this comes in a significant loss of a meaningful relationship. Or it may transpire in the loss of money or income. If someone persistently refuses the wake-up call, something may occur to compel them to wake up, such as a tragic accident or a significant health set-back. In other words, some people need to hit rock bottom before they "get it." You may have seen this happen, or you may have seen this happen repeatedly to the same person because a) others always come to the rescue and bail them out, or b) he or she is in denial, doesn't see the very clear signs, and will not take personal responsibility.

You are our brother's keeper, but only up to the line of demarcation determined by yourself. None of us is obligated to be sucked dry of our reserve of positive spiritual energy by someone who leeches from us, as a vampire would, causing us to sacrifice the goodness and unfailing fortitude within. You cannot help those who won't be helped, and you cannot save those who refuse to be rescued. Otherwise, we are enabling the spiritually blind who will conduct business as usual, like a dog chasing its own tail in circles. Disallow yourself from being manipulated or taken advantage of by someone who is masterful in the art of deception or who can, at the drop of a hat, give a persuasive performance worthy of an Academy Award. You'll recall this was touched upon in the chapter on being unselfish. Tending to yourself is not selfish, it's *self-preservation*. And it is necessary in order to maintain strength for being unfailing.

Where being human is concerned, give yourself credit for showing up, being involved, and putting forth effort to be good and to do good things. We all have bad days as well as great days when it seems like we are especially lucky or feeling great. And yet some of us, like the psychic among us, may be especially sensitive. When we are easily overwhelmed or labeled anti-social for desiring to retreat in isolation, good days may be fewer and farther between, and bad days become the norm. We may become worn and fatigued for having low energy. We may become irritated by others' demand and requests. And we may succumb to temptation, or addiction, for making us feel better temporarily in an act of self-medication. In the worst-case scenario, we vent our frustration on others irrationally, or we may turn it inward and self-destruct.

Such was nearly my situation, as I previously discussed. But I was somehow able to resist taking my own life. Unfailing is an unyielding resolve in the face of adversity. But when we struggle with low or poor self-esteem and unhappiness for years on end, continuing onward with any form of momentum is nearly impossible. I take solace in knowing that my brother is in a place where all his outstanding questions about the world's inequities have been answered.

Some may equate the concept of "unfailing" with its antithesis, that is, being a "quitter" if you falter or fail. But it is sometimes wise to know when to walk away if your time, energy, and attention is best directed elsewhere. To commit to your spiritual calling is to be unfailing. This requires a commitment of discipline to persevere in the interest of a good and just cause that will supersede one's own contributions over time. What this infers is that we may instigate a grand movement, cause, or shift that will be honored and perpetuated by others long after we have departed this world.

Part 3

Service to Others

Chapter 20

Spiritual Stations

In consideration of Love's Foot Rules in totality, it occurred to me that each entry might have varying degrees of significance according to our individual stations in life. We all possess gifts and talents, and those most fortunate among us have been able to parlay those traits into a vocation, or job, or an avocation, or hobby. But, as you well know, we also all have spiritual gifts and talents as well, though these may be less obvious or apparent, and, thus, perhaps more challenging to discern. Our spiritual gifts and talents will most likely correspond with our individual life stations. These life stations are usually preordained and tend to be those offices to which we feel called beginning in early childhood. Think of the person who, as a child, could brighten others' moods by smiling or laughing, or could grant insights of wisdom well beyond their years in keeping with the time-honored adage, "out of the mouth of babes."

I have identified 12 categories that might define one or more of your personal stations in life, and also those of your clientele as a practicing psychic. This list is not all-inclusive nor is it exclusive of any additions. I selected these stations in keeping with common themes I have noted in others who are engaged in the act of "becoming," and are aligning with their true calling. See if you can correlate your predispositions and interests with one or more of the following categories.

1. **Ambassador.** An ambassador has strong people skills for serving as a representative. He or she is naturally gregarious, with an open, energetic personality. This is the type of person who serves as a wonderful host or hostess, making you feel welcome, comfortable, and at home. The ambassador uses gentle and non-offensive humor, and will poke fun at themselves, particularly if there is a communication gap for being "new" to a foreign situation or navigating the cultural competency of an unfamiliar social setting. However, the ambassador is quick to learn the customs and nuances of a culture, or subculture, and will outwardly demonstrate his or her new understanding in an act of gracious goodwill.

   One on one, the ambassador will devote quality time to conversation with genuine interest in others' backgrounds, life path, family, and skills. The ambassador is consistent in his or her conduct, showing no bias, no prejudice, and no preferential treatment when interacting with others. The ambassador is poised and confident in representing people, places or things with great reverence and articulate knowledge. Spiritually speaking, the ambassador is a role model in setting an example for others to emulate without a need to amplify their own ego or draw attention to his or her accomplishments.

   The Love's Foot Rules most suited to the ambassador station are likely to be: Kind, Humble, Patient, Truth-loving, and Unfailing.

2. **Artist/Entertainer.** The individual who identifies with the artist or entertainer station was probably a child prodigy, demonstrating a preternatural talent at an early age. The artist or entertainer marches to the beat of a different drummer, and sees the world from an uncommon perspective and logic, almost as if going about life wearing a pair of unique lenses through which to interpret their surroundings. This person is keenly aware of details and incorporates these nuances in their work. This includes the beauty and humanity in all they survey as well as the tragedy and heartbreak. In all likelihood, the artist or entertainer has experienced great loss and tremendous pain, and can mask his or her depression by channeling it effectively into their art, music or performance. This person may require expansive amounts of time alone to engage with the creative process, retreating and seemingly becoming withdrawn during these times. As such, the artist or entertainer may not always be the most reliable for being absorbed in their total immersion and consistently losing track of time. This may cause those close to the artist or entertainer to feel exasperated or offended until all is restored and forgiven upon witnessing the fruit of their creation.

The artist or entertainer is deceptively sensitive, meaning, he or she may not reveal their true feelings and inner nature except to a very few confidantes. This individual may be a deep thinker and a private person to the point of appearing antisocial. In compensation, it is the artist or entertainer who best expresses him or herself through their creative output (as opposed to conversation). And when they do, what they have manifested tends to strike a universal chord for the way others react and respond. They may both inspire and incite strong reactions with their work. The artist or entertainer may even be heralded and lauded for their unusual vision, which nourishes their creative spirit and encourages them to continue creating.

The Love's Foot Rules most suited to the artist/entertainer station are likely to be: Long-suffering, Patient, Truth-loving, Endurance, Faith, and Unfailing.

3. **Caregiver/Caretaker.** The caregiver or caretaker is often thought of in the all-encompassing, generic role of "nurse." That is not to suggest that this station is exclusively for tending to others' ailments or physical well-being; this person knows some psychology as well. This is the individual that everyone historically looks to as the one who will "make it all better." The caregiver or caretaker is often a female who is naturally inclined to be a nurturer. Some may even actually refer to her as "mom" or "grandma" though there is no blood relation.

The person who occupies this station subconsciously operates on the level of "mother's intuition" as it pertains not just to immediate family but to friends, neighbors, and even strangers in the community. The caregiver or caretaker has a remedy to suit nearly every situation, be it dispensing advice and words of wisdom, or whipping up a specialty in the kitchen that is sure to bring soothing and nourishing comfort when served up piping hot. Additionally, this individual heeds a calling for feeling as though he or she is not only loved but needed for what it is they have to offer others, and this is deeply fulfilling.

The caregiver or caretaker may not realize it, but he or she is a natural-born empath, someone so sensitive that they not only accurately intuit someone's hurt, they also

210

literally feel it as well. This will tend toward the caregiver or caretaker taking on another's emotional pain, which may occur in conjunction with someone's physical distress. The caregiver or caretaker will also draw from their own experiences—which may have been painful and traumatic—in order to care for others. He or she may selflessly adopt the role of the devoted child who tends to the abusive sibling, or difficult parent, as that individual is dying and has abandoned all resources due to alienating others.

The Love's Foot Rules most suited to the caregiver/caretaker station are likely to be: Long-suffering, Unselfish, Patient, Endurance, and Unfailing

4. **Collaborator.** The person who identifies with collaborator as a life station is the epitome of team player. This individual may even have an eye, or an ear, for talent and can unite a group effectively by converging the very best of what each member has to offer with a great vision for the final outcome or product. Having said that, the collaborator has a keen sense for variables and diversity in personalities as well as intuiting what each can contribute. This person is a matchmaker of sorts when it comes to convening a group project or mission, singling out the very best individuals for their respective assignments. The collaborator may even challenge someone to step outside a comfort zone for envisioning an individual's potential.

The collaborator is also someone who has great flexibility in terms of a willingness to adjust the timeline or trajectory of the mission in keeping with the values and opinions of others. This requires the collaborator to be an effective listener, able to distill sometimes emotional or impassioned information to its purest form of sentiment before reiterating what has been said and heard. However, this does not mean that the collaborator loses sight of the end goal, only that he or she is able to adapt the tweaks and adjustments of others within the context of the bigger picture. When conflict arises, the collaborator is also a great mediator, supporting those in disagreement to see the opposing perspective and working to find compromise on common ground. Finally, the collaborator doesn't view him or herself as the reason for team success; he or she always sees themselves as part of the whole, albeit an integral and necessary part.

The Love's Foot Rules most suited to the collaborator station are likely to be: Kind, Free from covetousness, Humble, Pure in thought, and Truth-loving

5. **Communicator.** The individual who identifies with the communicator station is a powerful presence. He or she has an uncanny ability to connection with other people; to hone in on their personalities and backgrounds in order to establish common ground; and to keep a finger on the pulse of what's socially or spiritually relevant to each person. He or she also has an amazing memory for detail relevant to the discussion at hand. Because of this, the communicator is especially able to blend in virtually any social setting for having a worldly knowledge base that grants him or her the ability to converse with just about anyone on just about any topic. This is not to suggest that the communicator possesses a "gift for gab"; oftentimes the absence of communication is, in and of itself, an equally important and compelling communication all its own. Thus, the communicator understands the adage "silence is golden," and also comprehends the significance that being a strong communicator also requires one to be a good listener.

The communicator may have an affinity for vocations or avocations that encompass work as a writer, journalist, or impassioned and persuasive speaker. But the communicator could also infuse his or her opinions and beliefs in poetry or song lyrics as well. This approach may reach a broader, more diverse listening audience. The individual in the communicator station understands the use of humor and subtle satire to get the point across, such as in an animated or drawn cartoon, comedy sketch, or storytelling parable, like Aesop's Fables. This is most cleverly rendered with skill that allows for individual interpretation and is without sarcasm or the targeting others with the sole intent to offend. As such, the effective communicator is more likely to be revered than reviled.

The Love's Foot Rules most suited to the communicator station are likely to be: Truth-loving, Endurance, Faith, Hope, and Unfailing

6. **Healer.** The healer is a station that shares similarities with that of the caregiver/caretaker. But whereas the latter station is more about tending to others' immediate and long-term physical and emotional needs on an ongoing basis, the healer is naturally empathic and intuitive, emphasizing one's physicality and how the body's organs should collaborate in concert. In fact, some may refer to the person who identifies with this station as a "medical intuitive." This means the healer possesses the innate ability to gauge someone's physical ailment and route out the source of pain merely by looking at that person. This person readily senses when physical disharmony overtakes unison. The healer may also visually discern "healthy" or "unhealthy" colors associated with areas of the human body, and such descriptions may incorporate use of colors

correlating with the body's seven chakras or energy centers. The healer understands that he or she is the vessel through which healing energy flows in the manner of saying, "It doesn't come from me, it comes *through* me."

The healer may take to learning energy work and healing modalities naturally, such as becoming a skilled reiki master; but the healer may also possess raw talent that allows him or her to apply a unique holistic approach to treating someone without training. The wise healer recognizes the value of blending traditional medical treatment with alternative treatments, creating a personalized balance. Thus, the healer never denies someone access to traditional options nor claims to be the sole option. Instead, the healer provides the person being treated with a range of choices to be considered, allowing the individual to make an informed decision, and determine the proper path that makes the most sense personally. In additional to using their hands and intuition, the healer may also be a naturopath, with a keen understanding of the medicinal and nutritional value of plants, spices, roots, herbs, and plant-based oils, and how plant properties can be mixed into recipes for healing and strengthening remedies. It is of utmost importance that the healer tends to his or her mental-emotional, physical, and spiritual well-being in order to be of optimal service.

The Love's Foot Rules most suited to the healer station are likely to be: Humble, Unselfish, Patient, Endurance, and Faith.

7. **Historian.** The historian station may also be thought of as a librarian, archivist, and genealogist. This person is passionate for preserving documents, artifacts, and relics of the past. As a special focus, the historian values the

importance of educating others—especially the youth of upcoming generations—to hold appreciation and respect for the culture, the struggles, and the triumphs of those who lived before us. When we forget our history, we're liable to repeat the same mistakes unless we learn from them. The historian grants this perspective and aids us to mark our progress and see how far we've truly come.

The historian is also attuned to individuals on a personal level, and has the ability to offer insight that may be unconsidered by someone struggling to see the forest for the trees. The ability to console draws not only from the historian's knowledge of human behavior but also from a working knowledge of spiritual behavior. The historian understands that some of the same errors and issues experienced by someone—which tend to loop repeatedly without resolve—may have roots beyond the present timeframe. Thus, the historian has a grasp of how past lives may affect our present lives in ways that may be confusing unless and until the circumstances are laid bare and explained in a straightforward yet compassionate way. This is a select area of expertise for some historians who are privileged with an intuitive understanding for connecting the dots, so to speak, when someone's life cycles feel as if one is on a hamster wheel. When perspective is finally granted, unhealthy patterns may be discarded and longstanding cycles may be broken.

The Love's Foot Rules most suited to the historian station are likely to be: Long-suffering, Kind, Unselfish, Patient, and Endurance.

8. **Leader/Advocate.** Like the ambassador and communicator, those in the station of leader and advocate are highly effective in expressing themselves to others. But

oftentimes, this individual becomes so passionate about his or her beliefs that the leader and advocate leads with the heart more so than with the head. People best suited to this station become involved in their respective community as politicians, social workers, and human rights activists. This is because oftentimes the leader and advocate has come up the hard way through tough times of their own. But they have overcome their life obstacles, and have found success or contentment. As a result, they do not wish to see others suffer as they once did. So strongly does the person who occupies this station believe in fulfilling their purpose, that he or she is willing to make the ultimate sacrifice in order to ensure that others will enjoy equal rights, freedom, and prosperity in the future.

The leader and advocate has an innate sense of justice and appreciates the altruism that comes from upholding the truth. He or she is determined to illuminate the truth by publicly calling out liars and hypocrites, especially where others' rights are being violated. Not only might this individual have had personal experience with such hardships, he or she may also have a friend or a close family member that has been abused or manipulated by inequities in a system designed to support them. This may include minorities and immigrants, people of diverse faiths, people with mental or physical disabilities, and the elderly (particularly those with dementia). In addition to human rights issues, the leader and advocate may also hold concern and intolerance for injustices committed against living creatures of all kinds as well as the environment. The true leader and advocate has a disdain for power, wealth or celebrity for being free of ego; yet this individual also realizes he or she possesses a powerful, persuasive, and articulate voice that will call many to action to join forces with his or her mission.

The Love's Foot Rules most suited to the collaborator station are likely to be: Humble, Unselfish, Pure in Thought, Truth-loving, and Unfailing.

9. **Muse.** The person who identifies with the station of muse is a curious individual. The muse may often be considered off-beat, quirky or even a tad eccentric. The muse perceives the world from a unique logic and unusual perspective, viewed through multi-filtered lenses. Because the muse lives in so rare and unconventional a manner, he or she may be an object of fascination, attracting a broad array of individuals who find the muse refreshing and irresistible. The muse is an avid patron of the arts and is seemingly immersed in the creative process across multiple disciplines throughout each day. He or she is in perpetual motion to real or imagined music, is often witty and insightful, and is drawn to the details others usually overlook for being distracted by the "big picture."

He or she may also hold great influence over others but in an almost subliminal manner. The muse may serve as a source of inspiration for those who are so intrigued that they desire to emulate or pay tribute to him or her after a fashion. By the same token, the muse has an amazing eye and ear for identifying the gifts and talents of others. The muse instinctively knows what will best suit his or her protégé, and takes great delight in experiencing the excitement of someone uncovering dormant gifts and talents, and bringing them to full fruition. The muse intuitively knows how to balance what it is that a protégé should be exposed to in terms of fueling inspiration, and striking the appropriate chord between coach and mentor.

The Love's Foot Rules most suited to the muse station are likely to be: Kind, Free from Covetousness, Patient, Faith, and Hope.

10. **Teacher/Facilitator.** Like the muse, the teacher and facilitator may also serve as a source of inspiration for others. But where the muse offered encouragement from the background and at arm's length to avoid exerting too much interference on the creative process, the teacher/facilitator is actively engaged. The person who identifies with this station has likely always had an interest in helping and supporting others' acquisition of knowledge through a variety of learning opportunities. This could have started out as a babysitter, camp counselor, assistant coach, or after-school tutor. It is tremendously rewarding for the teacher and facilitator when a pupil grasps a concept, masters it, and then proceeds to apply it independently. Even if the teacher and facilitator is not themselves a biological parent, they nevertheless have many, many children—former students who recall them fondly for having had a profound impact on their lives.

The individual who identifies with this station appreciates that the wise teacher does not spoon feed information to his or her students but, instead, gently guides them, facilitating the process to a moment of discovery, whereby the student makes a connection and discovers the answer independently. This is why the teacher/facilitator's role will resonate so strongly for years afterwards. Additionally, the information and knowledge gleaned under the teacher/facilitator's instruction will be deemed so valuable as to be worthy of handing it down from one generation to the next. The teacher/facilitator is well organized and structured but does not necessarily function in a professional role at all. This individual may operate in a completely informal, but no less impactful, manner such as a doting grandparent or foster parent, an influential stranger, or a caring member of one's chosen family in adulthood.

The Love's Foot Rules most suited to the teacher/facilitator station are likely to be: Kind, Unselfish, Patient, Truth-loving, Faith, and Unfailing.

11. **Peacemaker.** The peacemaker almost unilaterally projects an aura of serenity. This tends to disarm others within the peacemaker's orbit, relaxing them and putting them at ease though they may be completely unconscious of the effect on them. The peacemaker instinctively knows how to diffuse a situation before it escalates and becomes explosive. This individual is the source of great and profound wisdom; this may stem from a wide range of personal experiences and exposure to many different types of personalities. Given this background, he or she usually knows just what to say in order to placate all parties embroiled in disagreement or disruption. As a result, the peacemaker is considered an outstanding listener and mediator who can summarize and articulate the standpoint of all perspectives before offering several viable solutions for both sides to reflect upon. Thus, the peacemaker does not necessarily purport to have all the answers but, instead, creates an opportunity for meaningful and insightful dialogue to transpire where, perhaps, there had been none at all.

The peacemaker's presence alone is not the reason why others call a truce or make amends; he or she merely facilitates a process of reconciliation as an impartial third party. Maintaining an objective attitude is an important component of the peacemaker so as to avoid accusations of partiality or favoritism. People who are naturally great and amazing parents are oftentimes great and amazing peacemakers. The peacemaker has a high moral standard and a strong code of ethics, and disallows others from lying, cheating, or manipulating a situation to their advantage and to the detriment of the opponent. To be most effective, the peacemaker must be adept at illuminating the truth efficiently and calling out the duplicity of others who are spurred on by self-gratifying motives.

The Love's Foot Rules most suited to the peacemaker station are likely to be: Patient, Pure in Thought, Truth-loving, Endurance, and Hope.

12. **Prophet.** The prophet is perhaps the most intuitive of all 12 stations. This person is highly sensitive and may be easily overwhelmed physically and emotionally for serving as a virtual tuning fork for all things seen and unseen. He or she may even feel cursed for having been an open channel all their lives, experiencing unexplainable or unsettling incidents tracing back to early childhood. In their youth, the prophet may have predicted tragedy or foreseen death, and this may have been frightening to both the individual as well as those immediately surrounding him or her. As a result, the prophet may have put forth great effort to deny and suppress their spiritual gift. Their special challenge is to rediscover, reawaken, and reclaim it on their terms and under their control. If the prophet can finesse his or her abilities—including the express refusal to receive any negative or harmful information—they are poised to be of extraordinary good service to countless others.

The prophet is under no obligation to utilize any or all of his or her talent; but the charitable side of this humanitarian personality will eventually yield to the calling. Of great importance is for the prophet to become acclimated to where, when, and with whom to use this aspect of their personhood, as he or she should only act on request and with permission (instead of approaching random strangers unexpectedly). Once this individual finds the balancing point between everyday life and responsibilities versus those moments in which the calling should be heeded, he or she will then be able to judiciously apply the gift of prophecy in a proactive manner. This may involve subtle or overt advisements in the form of gentle guidance for any domain of someone's life: relationships, employment, travel, children, relocation, and so on. The prophet recognizes that he or she is collaborating with a Higher Power and serves as a channel for the divine. Thus, serving in the prophet station should be an act of grace, free from the fear that anything other than loving communications with flow forth.

The Love's Foot Rules most suited to the prophet station are likely to be: Long-suffering, Humble, Truth-loving, Faith, and Hope.

Of course, you can hold more than one station, and chances are you identify with two or more already. For instance, I identify most closely with Communicator, Leader/Advocate, and Teacher/Facilitator. Your station identifications (sounds like a commercial break, doesn't it!) have the potential to shift in priority over time or to go dormant as new stations emerge depending upon where your life takes you, or what new passions or special interests emerge. There was a time when I would have thought I was most definitely Artist/Entertainer but now, not so much if at all. If you are uncertain about your personal station or stations, consult with a trusted loved one for insight. Think about the areas you've always felt drawn to. Reflect on what people have always told you you're a natural at and have a knack for doing. It may be that your station identity is so second nature that it's practically invisible for being so aligned with who you are and what you do.

People who know you best should be able to tell you without hesitation where your gifts and strengths lie. They should be able to readily offer you examples of occasions when you have openly manifested those gifts and talents, and how that has affected and positively impacted the lives of others. Conversely, this information may also merely validate and affirm what you were already thinking and feeling based on your own self-assessment. The sum-total of knowing this wisdom about yourself will be of glorious service to you as you move forward by crafting a plan to implement your spiritual stations as a practicing psychic in tandem with Love's Foot Rule.

Chapter 21

A Plan of Action

As has been discussed previously, our mindset and attitude have a direct impact on our physical well-being. Think about people who tend to be violent or impulsive, verbally and physically. Consider people who always seem to experience bad luck, as if a dark cloud is hanging directly overhead. Think about people who tend to be sickly on a consistent basis. Aren't these the folks who tend to be depressed, have poor or sarcastic attitudes, have addictions they won't own, and point the finger of blame at everyone except themselves? Not always, but most often this is true.

Bottom line is: You are what you attract, and you attract what you are. And this includes mental hygiene. In the manner that you can build a spiritual reserve within yourself (as was also previously discussed), so too can you create a spiritual deficit. Those who do so may even be doing it unwittingly as a byproduct of what they allow themselves to be exposed to. Our mental hygiene will be significantly comprised if we regularly curse or swear in anger and at others; play violent video games; watch gory horror movies; view pornography gratuitously; engage in vulgar, gross humor, especially if it demeans others; placate ourselves with a harmful addiction and justify it by lying to others and one's self; mentally, physically or sexual abuse others; and hold hateful, degrading thoughts for others who do not look and act as you do. This mindset is wholly toxic, and it cannot help but to fester and establish itself on a cellular level—not only by impacting and eroding one's mental hygiene, but by also instigating a cancerous poison that steadily causes ongoing physical ailments and deterioration. (And usually by this time of great need, such a person has alienated anyone in a position to help him or her.) Haven't you known someone who is elderly but because of a life-long positive attitude appears youthful and ageless? Conversely, haven't you seen the person who lives an unhealthy mental and physical lifestyle and is chronologically youthful but is physically broken and decrepit well beyond their years?

People who see the glass half empty tend to take their blessings and good fortune for granted, and thoughtlessly so. Others may presume an attitude of entitlement for feeling it is "owed" to them. But the universal news flash is that no one is promised or guaranteed *anything*. Your interpretation of what comes your way will poise you to take it in stride or cry the blues. You'll either portray yourself as a victim or become an activist of optimism, such as reflecting that brighter days are just around the corner.

Personally, I feel as though my good fortune comes with responsibility to be a good person and to set a good example. Just this morning, I was at the grocery store. Unpacking my cart to load my car, I noticed the purple toothbrush I had chosen off the store rack was still in the cart. I figured it fell out of one of the bags after I had checked out. I threw it in a bag, shut the trunk, and started to return the cart to the cart corral. But wait, I thought, what if I hadn't taken it out and put it on the checkout conveyor belt in the first place? That would mean it hadn't been paid for. There was a time when I would've been quietly pleased that I put one over on the corporation that was the supermarket, perhaps feeling it was compensation for overpaying inflated prices. Indeed, as a kid, there were a couple occasions when I actually did shoplift small items from my hometown grocery store.

But I'm a different and better person now. I opened the car trunk, dug out the receipt and checked—sure enough, no toothbrush had been rung up, or paid for. I marched back inside with it, approached the same cashier and explained what happened. She smiled, scanned it and asked for my total: a whopping $1.19, a miniscule amount. But it's not about the cost, it's about the principle of the situation. The person I am today is honest and truthful and knows that the deception would come back to haunt me somehow, some way if I decided to evade the truth and drive off with a stolen toothbrush.

The same concept of receiving a "return" on what you put out there is true of any aspect of our lives. It is universal law. Here's an example of how this might play out in real-time. On one of my long, afternoon walks, I entered a path through a wooded area. Midway, I always come to a very large, protruding boulder. I know it sounds nuts, but I always touch the boulder as I pass it and send it good vibrations. I figure it's been around for eons and has been witness to lots of transformations. I just want to let it know that someone notices it, and I recognize it in a tangible way.

One day, as I made my way toward the boulder, I noticed some young kid sitting on the rock—*my rock*! He was seated in a cross-legged position, almost like a yoga Lotus pose, with his eyes closed. He appeared to be meditating. As I walked by him, I jokingly remarked, "Hey, you're on my rock." He opened his eyes and smiled. I explained to him what I shared in the preceding paragraph about my "relationship" with the boulder and my spiritual affinity for it. He seemed interested and we engaged in a discussion about our respective paths. I introduced myself and he, likewise, did the same.

I learned that he is from Venezuela originally and that his name, Eric, is an Americanization of his given name because he felt "Eric" was easier to pronounce. We had a great, if impromptu, discussion about life and I shared with him many aspects of my personal evolution, which I've related previously in chapters of this book. I was impressed with Eric's wisdom and perspective, and I told him I thought he was much further along in his understanding than I was at 19 (his age then). I gave him my contact information if he wished to follow up and we parted ways.

Shortly afterwards, I received a message from his mother online. She wrote to tell me how excited Eric was to meet me and that she was intending to purchase one of my spiritual books for him to read. I told her not to bother with buying a book; I'd be happy to give him a book and personally inscribe his copy to him. She was delighted, telling me how much she loved to read and that this might encourage him to start reading again. At a prearranged date and time, I walked over to the adjoining development where Eric and his mother lived and dropped off the book. I had a nice chat with them both and discovered Eric's mother and I have similar spiritual belief systems.

Later that night, I heard from Eric, who thanked me by saying, "Knowledge is one of the best gifts someone can give." As he progressed through the book, he would chime in with experiences. We're on a roll, I thought. Hopefully, I was inspiring and motivating him, something his mother insinuated was much needed in his life. I smiled when he wrote, "Your book is amazing. It helps shine light on how to be happy, not to mention your interpretation of the world is pretty much awesome and realistic; not just some hippie mumbo-jumbo." So, you see, heeding the spiritual call to serve others, like Eric, is a matter of active engagement and not passive reception. It is this active engagement that will aid you to determine a plan of action and how best to apply your own gifts.

If you are reading this book, you are probably already working as a practicing psychic or are seriously considering making that leap of faith. As a byproduct of the work, you have the potential to meet any number of "Erics" if you haven't already. They will come in the form of people seeking information— wisdom, knowledge, or spiritual insight. Most often, they are on the precipice of a breakthrough themselves. Or, they are trying to make sense of their life history and all they've endured. Though they may be unaware of its totality in the moment, they are likely to be very much aware of a shift occurring in and around themselves. As there are no rules regarding personal awakenings, these folks will be a diverse age range as well as of varying ethnicities and backgrounds.

You are empowered to employ your psychic talents to identify the spiritual stations of each person whom you mentor. In this manner, you may have any number of wards whom you take under your wing until they are ready to take wing themselves. If this is your calling, incorporate it into a plan of action. Your plan of action is a living credo, a vision for who you aspire to be and what you desire to be doing. Mentoring others may well fit within that plan, and it is heartening to see others perpetuate the good and great influence you've imbued upon them.

Your plan of action may include balancing your psychic work with other modalities in order to sustain a viable income. You may be operating between being a psychic and other practices such as reiki and massage, for example. As part of your plan of action, you will wish to carefully delineate those good efforts from your psychic work. There is great potential for spill-over or bleed-over between them. That is, as you are giving reiki or massage to a client, it is quite conceivable to also be receiving psychic impressions about the individual. However, a psychic reading is not why your client is there; he or she is there for a different service. As such, the ethical thing to do is give the client the right of first refusal. You might say, "As I'm working on you, I feel as if I'm picking up on some intuitive information. Would you like me to share it with you or set it aside and continue what I'm doing?" In that respect, you permit the client to accept or decline.

Your plan of action may involve the desire to evolve into areas of specialty. As was mentioned before, you might have an interest in animals and want to develop that in order to offer pet readings. Taking that a step further, you may wish to hone your abilities in order to serve as a medical intuitive for animals by routing out the source of their pain, and being the interpreter about the health issue between them and the owner. If you are adept at using cards for readings, you may wish to invest meditative thought into creating your own deck as others have done. If you are the artistic type, you might illustrate your own cards or partner with an artist to do it for you. If you have an interest in astrology or use numerology to guide your psychic work, consider evolving that into creating charts unique to each client. An interest in rune stones and crystals could be developed into a presentation, workshop, or handbook for beginners.

Interfacing with children and teens was discussed previously and I believe this is a greatly overlooked demographic when it comes to spiritual giftedness, and education and support of such. If there are yoga studios, wellness centers, or natural food stores in your community that offer kids' classes, there might be an opportunity to interest young folks in a discussion group about paranormal experiences or to discuss psychic development practices. In keeping with the theme of children and teens, the opioid epidemic has claimed the lives of countless individuals, including a lot of teenagers and young adults. If you have been personally affected by this, or if you feel a special compassion for those who have been, you may wish to specialize in empowering people grappling with this struggle. You may also wish to specialize in supporting grieving families who have lost their loved ones through your mediumship abilities.

The other end of the spectrum is if you feel called to the geriatric population. You might want to develop skills in grief counseling using your psychic insights, particularly if you've been fortunate enough to have had glimpses of the other side or know enough about it from channeling other people's loved ones who are already there. It's amazing how beneficial this can be for clients who worry over whether they made the right decisions in the best interest of their elderly parent, for example. On several occasions, I believe I have connected to the soul energy of individuals with Alzheimer's disease who were mute and seemingly unaware. It's fascinating as they have a foot in both worlds. The feedback I provided was enormously comforting to concerned family members.

On other occasions, I have channeled what I believe to have been a benign extraterrestrial presence. This has been done in groups of people who have, themselves, had UFO sightings and other related experiences. I can tell you it was utterly unlike anything I have previously experienced. Though the presence was not threatening in any respect, he did take control to the point of—despite my eyes being closed—answering questions before they were asked, explaining why certain individuals experienced what they had (and in detail), and granting profound perspectives using phraseology that was not my own. There is likely to be at least one UFO interest group headquartered in your state. If this is something that intrigues you, you may wish to explore how you might crosswalk your psychic skills with aiding and educating the UFOlogists local to you. It could lead to some truly fascinating perspectives.

Where working with people is concerned, you may discover that your projections for clients' future pathways are frequently spot-on. You may wish to consider channeling your ability to give advice that comes to fruition into intuitive life coaching. In that respect, you'd be using your psychic abilities to proactively collaborate with clients by drafting plans for how to make improvements or achieve goals that have historically been procrastinated. Intuitive life coaching would be a perfect alternative for people who desire to blend professional advisement with a more spiritual or open-minded approach. In all likelihood, this guidance will address strengths and weaknesses forecasted by the three domains of which I spoke earlier: mental-emotional, physical, and spiritual. Special certification may be required in order to be accredited, so research this prior to pursuing this possibility.

Similarly, if you have a special interest in the romantic aspect of your work, as it pertains to insights on romantic chemistry and relationships, you may wish to evolve that specialty into psychic matchmaking. It is sure to be extremely popular given how frequently romance is an area asked about, particularly by female clientele. I have often thought that paranormal singles dating is long overdue, if only like-minded singles could be connected. You could host singles' events and social gatherings by which you use your psychic gifts to match one person to the other. These events could also involve paranormal- or intuitive-themed games and tests designed to have fun and create comfort levels such that people have a forum in which to get to know one another. Evolving this further could lead to an app or web site of your own creation, serving your community and beyond. It has tremendous potential, even on a smaller scale.

As you cultivate a reputation for outstanding psychic practices, you may find yourself the recipient of invitations to be interviewed for online podcasts or videos. If you feel comfortable with this media format, and you are articulate and enjoy chatting with others, your plan of action may call you to develop your own podcast. Hosting a regular program will reach greater numbers of interested individuals from outside your immediate community. You could offer psychic readings and predictions, and you could invite others to participate as special guests, authors, or co-hosts. You could designate specific episodes of certain days of the month to specific topics, or you could have theme shows—the format is entirely of your creative design. You might just discover that you truly enjoy the ability to reach and teach any number of listeners, as well as acclimating those who are uncertain to feel at ease to openly discuss their experiences.

I know intuitive individuals who draw upon their spiritual connections to channel when painting or creating crafts and jewelry. If you are similar, you might manifest amazing handmade artifacts as part of your plan of action. Many people enjoy acquiring unique, one-of-a-kind items, especially if you accompany them with an explanation of how you were inspired to create them, or distinguish each piece with a description of its intended purpose and how you infused its composition with elements to enhance that intended purpose. Such sidebar offerings could be a highlight of your web site and social media platforms, especially if you use or wear your own work as a subtle advertisement.

Above all else, it is imperative that you stay grounded and honor a code of ethics as you move forward and evolve your gifts in a plan of action. This book is intended to offer a framework of practical and ethical standards where none have formally existed previously. I'd like to conclude with seven guiding principles, fundamental tenets distilled to bullet points for your consideration.

1. **Love what you do.** If you don't find it fascinating and inspiring, it's time to evolve your plan of action, or find something else to do. If you become stagnant or jaded, it will manifest by deteriorating the quality of your

work. Find wonderment and joy in all that is mystical about being a practicing psychic. It is truly magical.

2. **Honor confidentiality.** You are not a doctor, psychologist, marriage counselor, or mental health therapist but you will find yourself dispensing similar advice. Hold yourself accountable to standards similar to the Health Insurance Portability and Accountability Act (HIPPA) by not revealing a client's personal information outside of a private one-on-one session. You may share anecdotes, such as in this book, in a generic way while preserving anonymity but do not share anyone's real name and story without his or her express permission.

3. **It's not about the money.** What you need will come to you as you need it if you are honorable in your practices and abide by the integrity to which you have committed. Don't compromise yourself out of desperation by accepting opportunities you would ordinarily decline because you need to make money. Make a living doing something else until you can shift into psychic work to earn the majority of your income.

4. **Do gratis work.** Extend yourself to others where and when you feel so called. You cannot be all things to all people, but you can serve some of them in your own way of making a charitable contribution. Do it not because it reflects well on your reputation but because it's the right thing to do. This is the proper response to honoring your psychic gifts.

5. **Illuminate the truth.** You will be required to have some very challenging, delicate, and perhaps uncomfortable discussions with clients on any number of sensitive subjects. Choose your words carefully and considerately. Remember that people can take quite seriously what you say, and the way you say it can have a profound and lasting impact. You can help to heal using honesty tempered with diplomacy.

6. **Be authentic.** There are no pretenses or expectations that you be anyone other than who you are. If you fabricate a façade that is deliberately odd or eccentric, you contribute to an unhelpful stereotype about psychics. The excellence of your work and your pleasant and calming personality is a dynamic combination that will generate wonderful word of mouth about your reputation. Nothing more is needed.

7. **Be an influencer.** Be mindful of mentoring others by identifying their gifts and talents, and encouraging them as much as possible. Nothing is more gratifying than to have served as someone's teacher, and watching as he or she spreads their wings and takes flight on their own. It will be an honor to know them as a friend and colleague.

You will continue to define your identity as a practicing psychic. As you do, you may also add to, or adjust, these guiding principles. If, at any time, real life should get in the way, and priorities and obligations cause you to set aside your practice, you can always come back it. Just like riding a bike, you might feel a bit rusty at first before grasping the hang of it all over again.

In the interim, I trust this volume will have served as a touchstone of sorts, especially if you've been operating in solace and without concrete guidance, as I once was. As much as I have learned, there's been an equal amount to unlearn. For me, there wasn't any roadmap with directions for traveling a path into the unknown. I hope this book has been that roadmap for you. Your career is truly what you make of it. If you go forth fearlessly, stand in the light of truth, and use your gifts for the betterment of others, the Universe will beam broadly upon you. I promise.

About The Author

William Stillman is an internationally known, award-winning author of 10 special needs parenting books including *Autism and the God Connection, The Soul of Autism*, and *The Autism Prophecies*, a trilogy that correlates aspects of autism with metaphysical themes. Stillman's work has resonated with parents, professionals, and persons with autism internationally, and has received endorsements of praise from bestselling authors and spiritual pioneers Gary Zukav, Carol Bowman, Dean Hamer, and Larry Dossey. To date, his books have been translated in four languages.

Stillman's spiritual work led to him contributing a week of daily reflections for the 2009 edition of *Disciplines: A Book of Daily Devotions,* and creating a training module for The Thoughtful Christian, a Web-based resource organization. His book *Conversations with Dogs: A Psychic Reveals What Our Canine Companions Have to Say (And How You Can Talk to Them Too!)* was published in 2015 and a new edition was printed in 2018 by Haunted Road Media. *Under Spiritual Siege: How Ghosts and Demons Affect Us and How to Combat Them*, about spiritual warfare with negative energies, was published in 2016, and his book, *The Secret Language of Spirit: Understanding Spirit Communication in Our Everyday Lives*, was released in 2017. In 2018, *The Secret Language of Spirit* was named a finalist in the National Indie Excellence Book Awards.

Additionally, since 1989, Stillman has coauthored six bestselling and critically-acclaimed books on *The Wizard of Oz*, most recently *The Road to Oz: The Evolution, Creation, and Legacy of a Motion Picture Masterpiece*, which won the 2019 National Indie Excellence Book Award in its respective category.

Stillman has worked professionally as a psychic medium and spiritual counselor since 2004. His accuracy in discerning the truth and making predictions that come to fruition has been acclaimed by his clients as truly extraordinary. He is regularly consulted on missing person and unsolved homicide cases. He also volunteers his time as an investigative resource to the Pennsylvania Paranormal Association.

Stillman has been interviewed on numerous radio shows of a paranormal nature including *Coast to Coast AM*, the most listened to overnight radio program in North America. He has twice been interviewed on the Web series *CharVision* by internationally renowned psychic medium Char Margolis, who called Stillman "really fascinating," and he has been a guest on the popular YouTube series *Swedenborg and Life*. Stillman has been a repeated guest speaker for Lily Dale Assembly near Jamestown, NY, the country's oldest and most revered spiritualist community.

Stillman's web site is: www.williamstillman.com and his Facebook page is: William Stillman Psychic Medium.

Other Haunted Road Media titles from William Stillman:

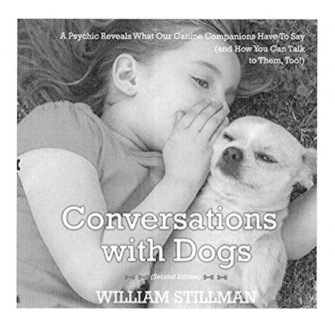

Have you ever wanted to know what your dog would say if he could talk? Now you can! Believe it or not, our canine companions have a lot to say beyond eat, drink, sniff, play and protect. In this fascinating new book, psychic William Stillman explores the dialogues he's had with dogs and reveals their inner most thoughts about their owners, their roles and the cycle of life. Also included is a step-by-step process for engaging your furry friends in a similar manner. Expect the unexpected as you prepare to enrich the relationship with your dog as a pet owner, friend and human parent.

Made in the USA
Middletown, DE
30 August 2021